A JOURNEY IN STONE

A JOURNEY IN STONE

CRAIG WEIGHTMAN

This impression 2015

ISBN 978 0 85318 491 1

All rights reserved. No part of this book may be reproduced or transmitted in any form or by any means, electronic or mechanical, including photocopying, recording or by any information storage and retrieval system, without permission from the Publisher in writing.

© Craig Weightman, 2015

Published by Lewis Masonic
an imprint of Ian Allan Publishing Ltd, Hersham, Surrey KT12 4RG.

Printed in England

Visit the Lewis Masonic website at www.lewismasonic.co.uk

Copyright

Illegal copying and selling of publications deprives authors, publishers and booksellers of income, without which there would be no investment in new publications. Unauthorised versions of publications are also likely to be inferior in quality and contain incorrect information. You can help by reporting copyright infringements and acts of piracy to the Publisher or the UK Copyright Service.

All illustrations © Craig Weightman

Front cover

Sculpture – 'Self Made Man' © Bobbie K. Carlyle *www.BobbieCarlyleSculpture.com*

CONTENTS

Acknowledgements	8
Preface	9
Introduction	17
Chapter 1 What is Freemasonry?	27
Chapter 2 The Rough Ashlar	43
Chapter 3 The Working-Tools of the First Degree	53
Chapter 4 The Working-Tools of the Second Degree	69
Chapter 5 The Working-Tools of the Third Degree	85
Chapter 6 The Perfect Ashlar	103
Chapter 7 King Solomon's Temple and Society	121
Chapter 8 The Illusion of the Self and the Truth of Interdependency	139
Chapter 9 The Transformative Symbolism of the Royal Arch	157

For Justine,
Oscar, Isabelle, and Molly,
who provide so much inspiration
in my daily life.

ABOUT THE AUTHOR

Photo: *Shaun Smith*

Craig Weightman grew up in Hinckley, Leicestershire and was educated at the University of Leicester, gaining a degree in Psychology and Computer Science. He was initiated into Freemasonry in 2003, and became master of his lodge in 2014.

Outside of his interests in Freemasonry, Craig is a lecturer in Computer Games Design and Computer Science at a College in Warwickshire. He also develops websites for businesses.

He lives with his family in Coventry.

ACKNOWLEDGEMENTS

I would like to take this opportunity to offer thanks to all of those people who have been so crucially helpful in the development of this book. To Philippa Faulks and the rest of the team at Lewis Masonic for believing in the work. To my father, Peter Weightman, for offering his support as my first editor and proof-reader. To the love of my life, Justine, who has been a pillar of support throughout, even though this book was being written during the early days of our newborn son, Oscar.

Lastly, I would like to thank Freemasonry itself, for providing me with the wonderful insights that gave me the inspiration to write this book.

PREFACE

Deciding to become a Freemason is a unique experience. For a start, you have probably not encountered very many Freemasons in your everyday life. There you are, going about your day-to-day business, perhaps having an inkling that there exists a society of people called Freemasons, but not knowing too much about them.

Then, one day, you perhaps discover that a person you have worked with for a while is a member of this Society. If you are on friendly terms, and you wish to know more about what the organisation actually is, a conversation on the subject naturally follows, and it is at this point that you might discover how interested in Freemasonry you actually are. This expression of interest is then perhaps followed by an invitation to one of the events which non-Freemasons are able to attend, usually a Ladies' Night, where the members of a Masonic lodge take their respective ladies to a dinner-dance that is arranged each year.

If you have heard anything about Freemasonry then up to this point that information has probably been replete with the various myths that have been spread into the wider world. These myths include that it is a secret society, that being a member secures special privileges and advantages in ordinary life, that the Freemasons are the secret shadow government that pulls the strings in political affairs, and that you have to be singled out and invited in order to join. This is just a short list of the kinds of myths and rumours that are circulating the globe regarding Freemasons.

It turns out that the conversation you have had with the newly-discovered Freemason has dispelled many of these rumours. The final one mentioned, that one has to be invited to join, is dispelled even further when you are informed that if you want to join then you have to express an interest in joining, as Freemasons cannot invite people to join because it is regarded as a Masonic offence.

This revelation sets your mind into action, and you find yourself asking whether you are really interested enough to want to join this organisation. You realise that the person you have questioned about Freemasonry hasn't actually said anything about what it is they actually do in their private meetings. They have mentioned that the Society gives a great deal to charity, that it has something to do with moral development, and that it is a Society for like-minded individuals, with an emphasis on initiation. They might even have mentioned that it derives its origin from the ancient mediaeval stone-guilds whose members used their working-tools as symbols and metaphors for moral development.

Having realised that your curiosity is certainly piqued, you decide that it might be a good idea to join and to see what it is all about. After all, the Society seems benevolent enough, and it seems thoroughly steeped in history and philosophy. You then fill in the application form after your new-found Masonic friend has agreed to propose you and you have met someone who is prepared to second you. You are also informed that your application will be subject to a ballot undertaken by the existing members of the lodge, a process where Freemasons apparently put coloured balls into a bag, and in which a white ball in the bag means yes, and a black ball means no. You are told that if there is just one black ball found in the bag at the end of the ballot then your application will be rejected.

You await the results of the ballot which, as it turns out, proves in your favour. You are then told that you must turn up to the lodge, on your own, at a particular time, and on a particular night.

The period of waiting, as you see the days tick down to event zero, is an interesting experience and, as the night approaches, your nervousness slowly increases. You realise that you are joining something that you don't really know anything about, and that, given all the myths about Freemasonry that abound in the world, perhaps you should have your sanity checked.

Nevertheless, the day dawns and, that evening, you make your way to the Masonic lodge rooms where your initiation is to take place. This first point of contact with the actual world of Freemasonry involves meeting someone standing outside a door. They appear to be wearing a smart suit and, bizarrely, a square apron, and some kind of light-blue collar. However, despite the strange dress of this Freemason, and the circumstances of the evening, this person puts you at your ease. Of course, the natural sense of nervous tension that you have been feeling within as a result of facing the unknown hasn't subsided, but you appear to understand that nothing bad is going to happen to you. You are told that what is about to happen has happened to every Freemason you will meet this evening, and that there is nothing to fear.

Every Freemason in the world has experienced a similar story to the one described above with regard to their entry into the Masonic Order. Pretty much everybody joins the organisation without the faintest idea what Masonic initiation is all about. It turns out that the nervousness generated by the mystery of what is about to be faced is crucial to the initiation process, as it helps one to genuinely face their fears, which is one of the particular qualities of any system of initiation.

Once a person has passed through the ceremony of their First Degree they have a tendency to feel that they have known the people that they have just met all their life. Everyone is so welcoming, and one feels a sense that one is part of something bigger than oneself, and that one has experienced something genuinely unique.

Of course, this first initiation is the first of Three Degrees, and the Freemason steadily progresses through all of them until they reach the stage of a fully-initiated Master Mason.

The Freemason might then decide that they wish to progress through the sequence of offices up to the the chair of the Master of the lodge.

If the Freemason is deeply interested in the subject of Freemasonry, and in understanding where such an organisation comes from, then they will usually undertake to study everything they can to shed light on the subject. After all, there is very little in Masonic ceremony that fully explains any context. This is something the Freemason has to find for themselves, and it is intentionally so, because the Masonic Initiate is encouraged to pursue a daily development of Masonic knowledge: the initiation ceremonies themselves are but springboards to the contemplative process.

If the Freemason delves deeply into what is written about the Craft they soon learn that the roots of the Order can be found reaching everywhere. Discovering Freemasonry sends one on a journey through the history of the world, and into finding out about ancient traditions of initiation that seem to promote one single message, no matter where these traditions are in the world.

The Freemason finds that the system of initiation that is expressed in Freemasonry is the descendent of more ancient traditions, and that the language of stonework is merely intended as an allegory for the deeper meaning that is being expressed. The message is disguised as such because it is only visible to the Freemason who is prepared to see it, after having developed their Masonic knowledge through their personal study to the point where they are able to join the dots, so to speak. In this way, the tradition of Freemasonry is a path to the revelation of a very deep secret.

However, one's time as a member of a Masonic lodge quickly reveals that there are three types of member, who regard Freemasonry in different ways. There are those who go to the meetings, mainly to meet other people, to enjoy the companionship and a good meal at the end of the meeting. These members are known in Masonic circles as knife-and-fork Masons, and it is a mystery to anyone else why they would sit through the ceremonies in the meetings simply to go to a meal. Thankfully, there aren't too many of the knife-and-fork kind of Freemason.

Then, there is the kind of Freemason who sees the Craft as a way of communicating morals and making good people better. These Freemasons spend time diligently learning the necessary words in order to take part in the ceremony. However, it is as if the total substance of the Craft is the learning of and performing of ritual to the best of one's ability. When observing these Freemasons, it is possible to find oneself wondering if they have delved deeper into the meaning of the Craft so that the words they are learning have context. This kind of Mason seems to make up the majority of the membership. These members appear to be happy with learning the ritual, enjoying their fellowship of the lodge, and being part of a charitable organisation which helps many causes throughout the world. This, of course, is fine. There is clearly a source of challenge and enjoyment for the membership of this type of Freemason.

Finally, there is the third type of Freemason. This type is similar in every way to the second type, but with one important difference. This type of member reads widely and deeply on the subject of Freemasonry, and passionately traces its development wherever it will lead them. In doing so, they find themselves educating themselves about a diverse range of subjects and traditions. On referring what they discover back to the symbols of the Craft, they begin to deepen their understanding of what Freemasonry actually is and what the nature of the secret is that it is leading the Freemason to discover.

As well as following a path of education to support their Masonic membership they spend time looking inward, at their own psychological development and at their own inner natures. The symbolism of Freemasonry, for these members, becomes a new way of thinking, which enables them to take a diverse range of topics and utilise metaphor to understand them better. Even in the passage of their own lives, they look at situations and then look to the language of Freemasonry to help them acquire insight.

Also, since they have spent some considerable time studying the subject of Freemasonry, they find that this helps them in learning and understanding the ritual of Freemasonry. When they deliver the various passages they have learned in the context of the ritual, their understanding helps them deliver it with feeling, to the benefit of the Candidate who is listening to it.

It is clear, then, that the third kind of Freemason appears to get the most enjoyment and the most benefit from their membership. It is as if they have taken a cup of cool refreshing liquid and, rather than feeling satiated by sipping from the cup, they drink deeply, feeling the liquid as it animates and refreshes the entire body.

It is therefore one of the aims of this book to help to turn the first kind of Freemason into the second kind of Freemason, and the second kind of Freemason into the third kind.

This book is the result of years of exploration by myself since I joined the Order of Freemasons in 2004. After following an identical story to the one expressed at the beginning of this preface, I found the process of initiation a truly transformative process. As soon as I could find out more about the Craft I did, and delved deeply into all of the books on the subject that I could find. As I read, I found a new interest in history, and a path to a deeper insight into the subject of comparative religion in which I was always deeply interested.

Throughout my life, even before my Masonic career, I would read everything I could about the different religions of the world. I had always been interested in the questions surrounding divinity, but felt unease that there are so many different religions in the world, each claiming to be the correct one. It seemed, to my mind, that none of them seemed to be confident in their expression of divine truth. However, it is clear that there is something deep within human beings that inspires inquiry into the nature of existence, and the fact that there are so many faiths with a similar thread running through them points to the fact that there is something to be learned from all of them. Therefore, I have always preferred to stand apart from any one faith, preferring the freedom to study the differences and similarities amongst all of them, confident that there is something out there, and that it could be found for oneself.

Upon entering the Craft, and cheerfully embracing the new course of study that had been laid before me, I found myself reading about a long tradition of systems that, in many ways, shared my view of the possibility of spiritual insight developed entirely under one's own steam. The system of initiation was designed specifically for this very purpose.

In discovering more and more about Freemasonry, I found that I had become part of something that suited me like a well-fitting glove: a system of allegory that veiled an initiation process that is as old as, and perhaps even older than, civilisation itself.

Since the subject of religion has been mentioned here in the context of Freemasonry encouraging an interest in it, it is important to stress that Freemasonry itself is not a religion. It has no dogma, no God specific to it, and no rules of conduct that are particular to Freemasonry. It is demanded that a person wishing to join has a belief in some kind of supreme being, but this is only because it is this kind of person who might derive the most benefit from the Order. What Freemasonry can be defined as is a philosophy and a way of thinking and living, in the non-religious sense. Of course, as has been mentioned, it does have the ability to deepen the understanding of one's pre-existing beliefs.

One of the interesting aspects of Freemasonry for me is its unique blend of placing an emphasis on both the development of the intellect and faculty of rationality on the one hand and the emotional and instinctive faculty on the other. These two angles are combined to help the Freemason search for the secrets that it states have been lost. Again, this is perfect for me, because I am trained in the sciences, initially in physics, and then in computer science and psychology. My way of thinking is nearly always steeped in logic and rationality, and this has been my approach in understanding the deeper insights offered by many religions. However, Freemasonry makes clear that reason alone is insufficient in uncovering what one aims to find, and that one must hone one's emotional insight as well.

It is important to remember that this book represents my particular insights into Craft Freemasonry, and to most effectively communicate it I have chosen the image of the crafting of stone to reveal a form within. Imagining the chipping away of stone to create a work of art that is revealed within is, I believe, the perfect analogy for expressing what Freemasonry sets out to do.

It is hoped that Freemasons will find this work very useful in helping them to deepen their understanding of the organisation of which they have become a member. However, it is also intended for the non-Mason.

As has already been mentioned, there are many myths and conspiracy theories circulating in the world. This modern age of the Internet allows the gathering of information at a far faster rate and, unfortunately, this means that myths and conspiracy theories also make their rounds faster.

Therefore, the other aim of this book is to help clear up such myths. The myth of secrecy about what Freemasonry is ought to have already been dispelled if you are a non-Masonic reader, as you are holding a book that reveals what Freemasonry is all about, written by a member of the Society. As you read, other myths will vanish, for instance the exclusivity of its membership.

Throughout history, people have been led to believe that Freemasonry is exclusive to the point of restricting its membership only to those who are specifically invited, or who are wealthy, or to men only.

The first of these three myths has already been dispelled at the beginning of this preface. The second myth, that only the wealthy and influential are allowed to join, can also be safely done away with. Whilst I have indeed met members who are very affluent indeed, I have also been in company of others who have come from all sorts of backgrounds and walks of life. Everyone is represented, even lowly college lecturers such as myself.

The third myth, that only men are allowed to join, is a popular myth in this post-feminist era. However, it is just that, a myth. Whilst Freemasonry does have its roots in a history where only males were allowed to join the Society, times have moved on. Nowadays, there are both male lodges and female lodges, and I myself know two members of a female lodge. However, in most cases, whether it is a male lodge or a female lodge, membership is restricted to that one particular gender, apart from a few exceptions. Whilst Freemasonry is very much male-dominated in the main, it cannot be denied that females are also allowed to participate in Freemasonry. This being the case, great care has been taken to ensure that the language used in this book is predominantly gender-neutral, so as not to convey the myth that the organisation is fraternal only.

After reading this book, whether you are a Freemason or a non-Mason, it is hoped that you will feel further enlightened on the subject. It is hoped that the Masonic readers will have a refreshed purpose to their membership where, perhaps, they weren't quite clear of one beforehand. The intention for the Masonic reader is to lead you to a process of discovery for yourself, so that you can test the claims of this book in your own life and membership. You may find that what you read in this book can indeed be backed up by your own experience. You may also acquire a deep insight of your own, which I have missed in my studies, or which has not been covered in this book.

My intention for the non-Mason is not just to dispel myths, however. It is also to educate you about what Freemasonry actually is and to provide some idea of the scope of its philosophical outlook. After you have read these pages, it is hoped that you might understand, better than I did when I started out, the deeper purposes of Freemasonry.

If you are a non-Masonic reader who is hoping to join at some time in the future, you may safely traverse these pages without the risk of spoilers. I have been very careful to omit details of the actual experience of initiation. I am very much a defender of the idea that the initiation ritual should be kept within the doors of the lodge, merely for the preservation of the profound experience it is intended to be. If people entered Freemasonry already understanding the details of what is to come, then the effect of the whole experience would be lost. A new Initiate is meant to feel apprehensive and is supposed to feel as if they are stepping into the unknown.

Of course, those who intend to join, and who will have read this book, will have an expectation of the kinds of symbols that they will come across. However, these are not necessarily spoilers and reveal nothing of the context of the total experience of the actual initiation ceremonies. What will happen, however, when you come across these symbols is that you will realise that you understand these symbols in a much deeper way when they are first introduced to you. With this in mind it is hoped that, rather than spoil anything for you, it will help to more quickly provide a context for your membership and deepen your enjoyment of the whole system.

Regardless of the angle from which you approach this book, it is intended, in general, to be informative and enjoyable.

INTRODUCTION

It is widely believed that Freemasonry began with the mediaeval stone-guilds. These guilds essentially behaved as a quality-control mechanism in the stone-working industry. To this end, the secrets and techniques of stonework were kept a close secret, accessible only to members of the guild.

It was important that members of the stone-guild kept the techniques imparted to them a secret and this meant that only those who could be proved as moral and honourable individuals could become apprenticed members. Morality would have been of primary importance for these operative masons.

To ensure that only members of the guild could access their meetings, and also gain work at building-sites, a system of secret handshakes and passwords was created for means of identification. These forms of recognition are still used today and, it must be stressed, are the only official secrets of Freemasonry.

Of course, in the mediaeval era, many people were illiterate and also very God-fearing. Therefore, in order to teach and maintain morality, the stone-guilds utilised a technique of moralising on the tools and techniques of stonework by using these everyday building elements as metaphors for moral concepts. The God-fearing stonemason was also reminded that God is always watching, and so one should maintain morality, wherever they are.

How did operative masons become what we now know as Freemasons? It is believed that, amongst the many members who actually worked stone, there were some members who were honorary in nature. These honorary members would not work stone, but would still be initiated into stone-guild lodges, and take part in their meetings. These members were called Free and Accepted Masons, or Freemasons for short.

Eventually, as the power of the operative stone-guilds waned, operative members would decline over time, leaving the honorary Free and Accepted members. Lodges would eventually be composed primarily of Freemasons, and it would seem that the focus on the craft of stonework was replaced by another craft, that of moral development. Indeed, Freemasonry is often called 'the Craft.' This, then, is how Freemasonry exists today.

This book examines Freemasonry in terms of being a club for self-development, which uses stonework as a metaphor for this purpose. It sees it as a society that encourages the member to look at their life as a stone block that is to be carved and shaped into something meaningful.

Upon entering Freemasonry, a new Candidate is intended to be seen as a stone taken from a quarry. As this stone is passed through the stonework process it is honed to a smooth stone block, to be included in a larger edifice or building.

If this quarried stone can be seen as representing the individual Mason, then the building it is intended for, being composed of similar blocks, can be seen to represent society as a whole. Therefore, the individual self-development talked about here, rather than being selfish, is intended to serve society as a whole. Just as each block plays a full role in allowing a building to stand, so the developed Mason has found how they can fully serve and support society as a whole.

The symbolic language borrowed from the stonework process consists mainly of the tools used. As mentioned above, it is to be imagined that these tools can be used to hone the Mason into something more useful for society. To give two examples: in stonework, the gavel, which is a small hammer-like tool, is used to knock off rough parts of a stone. In Freemasonry, this gavel represents the force of conscience. The chisel is used in stonework to smooth the stone further in its preparation for inclusion in the larger building. In Freemasonry the chisel represents education.

Freemasonry, then, is a journey, a journey that serves to sculpt a person into a more useful element of society. However, this journey requires a story to provide structure and also perhaps a little context.

The job of this context is undertaken by a legend which is set around the biblical story of the building of King Solomon's Temple. This building was believed in Old Testament times to be literally the house of God. The Temple was the home of the Ark of the Covenant, and was specially designed to be worthy of such a purpose.

Therefore, in Freemasonry, it can be seen that King Solomon's Temple can be treated as the ideal template for an ideal societal metaphor, where individual stone blocks come together to create a decent society.

Clearly God is central to the building of the Hebrew temple, so it is no surprise that God is mentioned during the story's telling. It is here that mention should be made of Freemasonry's further use of symbolic language to promote the tolerance of members coming from a diverse range of belief systems. So that a Mason of any religion can see the deity mentioned in the Masonic story as the deity of their own faith, the symbolic name for 'God' is 'The Great Architect of the Universe.' This is done so that the individual Mason can relate the moral teaching of Freemasonry to their own beliefs. The term 'Great Architect of the Universe' is often misconstrued by non-Masons to be a kind of Masonic God. However, this is not true, and is only a general term to be used to signify the deity in general.

Generally speaking, in English lodges the Bible is opened at every meeting. During initiations, obligations are taken on this document, and an alternative to the Bible may be used as required. Freemasonry directs a Mason to study the scripture of their faith in order to know, understand, and follow divine law. To account for diverse religious backgrounds, there is a general symbolic term which allows Freemasonry to talk about the central scriptures of all faiths in a single term. This general term is 'The Volume of the Sacred Law.'

Going back to where we mentioned the development of oneself to better serve society, it should be remembered that, as a stone is sculpted to fully serve its part in the upholding of a structure, so a Freemason is encouraged to understand how they can fully serve and support society. This objective requires self-knowledge, and the acquisition of this knowledge is a deeply personal journey. Therefore, Masonic ceremony is designed to reflect this personal journey, and Candidates are led through and directly experience a three-part symbolic story. It is usually down to the Mason to interpret this experience for themselves.

This book has been written for both Masons and non-Masons. For the Masonic audience it intends to help Masons better understand their Craft in terms of moral and personal development. For the non-Masonic audience, the book hopes to reveal what Freemasonry is all about and to help put to rest many of the rumours that have surfaced over the years.

In the book, you will follow the Candidate through Freemasonry and learn about some of the symbols that are utilised, with a focus on how they use the metaphor of stonework to encourage personal and moral development. We will move from the moment a Freemason joins until the point when they theoretically discover who they are and what they can offer society as a whole.

The structure of the book is organised so as to introduce the concepts of Freemasonry in some sort of logical order. Initially, in order to give the rest of the book some context, some time has been spent explaining what Freemasonry actually is in greater detail, placing the initiation tradition into its correct background. Such traditions can be found throughout human history, in fact since the time of prehistory. In the beginning, the initiation tradition was designed to prepare the tribal warrior or huntsman to enable them to face their fears and to overcome them.

Developing further, alongside the development of the world's religions, there has continued the tradition of initiation within a more spiritual context. Whereas the main and more public part of these religions were intended for the general populace, there also existed a more specialised version for those who were found to be sufficiently gifted. These specialised pathways were not administered in the same way as the esoteric side of the religions; instead, a system of Candidate-based ritual was used.

In these rituals, the Initiates would be taken through experiences which would bring home to them, in a dramatised way, the inner truths of their spiritual tradition. The ultimate truth that most of these esoteric traditions would centre on was that the human being was one with the divine. In fact, this single truth can be found in almost all of history's initiation traditions, no matter where in the world they can be found.

Indeed, even the more mainstream religions of the world have reflected this philosophy. In India, the spiritual texts would focus on the oneness between the world soul, Brahman, and the personal soul, Atman. It is therefore the pervasive nature of this concept that makes it so attractive. The central concept of the spiritual union between man and the divine has been reproduced in nearly every culture, no matter how far apart in time or geography. Perhaps therefore, this ultimate truth rests at the heart of humankind and of the universe at large.

It would seem, at first glance, that the stone-guilds would be an odd place to find the same spiritual philosophy. However, the stone-guilds were the keepers of great secrets that enabled the construction of wonderful edifices that would seem to defy the forces of nature in order to remain standing. The knowledge of how to do this was considered very special indeed. In fact, understanding the physical laws to be utilised at will was like understanding how the divine had constructed the universe. Therefore, to understand the science of construction was to have glimpsed the nature of the divine.

The stone-guilds were not alone in this. In ancient times, the Pythagoreans would place spiritual significance on the relationships between numbers. These relationships could be seen reflected in the world around them, and the very workings of the world seemed to be dependent on them. Even the Egyptians understood Pi and its relationship to the circular structures seen in nature. Therefore, this mathematical spiritual knowledge and its expression in the art of stonework and building can easily be linked to the divine revelation of initiation.

The stonemason, and then the Freemasons who descended from them, would therefore have imparted the same knowledge that neophytes in other traditions would partake of, and the Masonic Initiates would feel the union between themselves and the divinity behind the world.

After providing context, the book then moves on to the symbolism that is used to represent the Initiate when they first enter Freemasonry. This representation of a rough stone, freshly hewn from the Earth in preparation for the work of initiation, is the perfect place to start in a tradition that likens inner development to the crafting of stone. The representation is analysed in detail, and a picture is drawn of the particular faculties, which are to be improved as the Freemason moves through the regenerative process of Masonic ceremony. Importantly, where necessary, the metaphor of the rough stone or ashlar is framed in a modern interpretation.

The specific symbols on which this book focuses are the ones relevant to the crafting of stone, and therefore more directly understandable as symbols of transformation. These specific symbols are known as the working-tools. There are three sets corresponding to the Three Degrees of Freemasonry.

Having mentioned that there are Three Degrees of Masonry, there may be some confusion amongst both Masonic and non-Masonic readers alike caused by the fact that there seem to be more than Three Degrees in Freemasonry. The Scottish Rite of Freemasonry contains thirty-three Degrees, of which the Degrees that form the subject of this book are only the first three.

To clear up this confusion we should make it clear that pure Freemasonry consists of Three Degrees and the Holy Royal Arch, which used to be part of the Third Degree until it was made into a separate ceremony. The other Degrees of systems of Masonry, such as the Scottish Rite, are extra Degrees that further analyse the lessons of the ordinary Three Degrees of Craft Freemasonry. Once a Freemason has passed through the Third Degree they are a fully-initiated Mason, whether they have taken any of the other Degrees or not.

In the chapter immediately following the description of the rough ashlar we analyse the working-tools of the First Degree. The emphasis in the First Degree is on initiating the Candidate into the whole system of Freemasonry, and introducing them to what is expected of a Freemason once they have joined. The point of initiation is made very clear throughout this book; one doesn't simply join Freemasonry as one would join an ordinary club. One is initiated into Freemasonry, and this means a line is drawn under the life that has been lived prior to entering the lodge, at which point the new life of the Freemason begins.

The challenge of being a Freemason is to live one's life while aspiring to the highest moral virtues, and a person who becomes a Freemason undertakes to tread this very same path.

During the process of initiating the new Freemason into the Craft, the First Degree working-tools are presented to them. These tools represent the active crafting of the Self, and are the basis of any future Masonic growth.

The chapter on the Second Degree's working-tools takes the emphasis on active self-development and places it within the context of self-measurement and mindfulness of the Self. The Second Degree is representative of how the Freemason should proceed through life, and places a particular emphasis on the understanding of the hidden mysteries of nature and science. Where the theme of the First Degree is direct moral development, the theme for the Second is the intellect and rationality.

Each of the three tools of the Second Degree are purely tools of measurement, and are designed to emphasise that the Freemason should ever be mindful of their progress in the crafting of themselves. This progress is always measured against the guiding principle of the perfect ashlar, the smooth stone that represents the goal on which the Freemason sets their sights. As the Freemason moves further away from the path, the tools of the First Degree should continue to be utilised until the correct course has been regained.

Also, it is in the Second Degree that the inward journey of the Freemason is made apparent. As with the other initiation traditions of old, the Masonic Initiate is moving closer to the transcendent principle that lies at their very core.

In the final part of the crafting journey of the Freemason, the emphasis begins to shift from a focus on the Self to a focus on the wider context of Freemasonry. It is in the Third Degree where the Self is analysed and the emphasis on it reduced in favour of society as a whole. To reflect this shift in focus, the three working-tools of this Degree are all tools that are to be used in the wider context of the building-site.

By using the tools of the Third Degree, the Freemason begins to find their place amongst the world and to understand the true purpose of Freemasonry itself. Particular emphasis is placed here on understanding a spiritual interpretation of moral values, and a case is made for a transcendent origin of morality.

As previously mentioned, the guiding principle of Freemasonry is the perfect ashlar, and it is after detailing the Freemason's journey through the transformative properties of the working-tools of each of the Degrees that we come to describe this object. The ideal Freemason is described in some detail, but great care is taken to remind the reader that the journey towards the perfection which is represented by the smooth ashlar takes an entire lifetime, and that it is not humanly possible to achieve all of the necessary qualities in full splendour and in one person.

Of course, the perfect ashlar representing the Freemason has an intended purpose: that of becoming part of a grander building. In Freemasonry, this building is the most important building in the Old Testament, namely King Solomon's Temple. Some time is spent explaining the religious importance of the Temple and its purpose before embarking on its use as a symbol in the Craft. The particular symbol of King Solomon's Temple is then presented in three different interpretations of equal importance: as the representation of the universe at large, as the representation of the individual human being and, finally, as the representation of society. To help this discussion, a description of the formation of a Masonic lodge room is used. This is because a lodge room is designed to represent the temple at Jerusalem.

Moving on from the analysis of the journey of the Freemason, the point of initiation is returned to that of uniting the Self with a transcendent principle. In all initiation traditions, the Self is symbolically dissolved into the wider context of the divine, which in turn is distributed throughout the universe.

To assist this discussion, the illusion of the separate Self is introduced and logically analysed so that the truth of the unreality of what we take for granted as the Self becomes obvious. After achieving this aim, the idea of the natural interconnectedness of all things, including the members of society to each other, is introduced and discussed. Ultimately, this chapter provides the key to understanding the process of initiation as a philosophically spiritual practice.

In the final chapter, Freemasonry is confirmed as an heir to the tradition of initiation in an analysis of the Holy Royal Arch's Ceremony of Exaltation. This particular part of Masonic initiation is most obviously mystical in its make-up. In this chapter, a description of some of the story of the Exaltation Ceremony is included, so that the intended meaning of the symbolism can be properly explained. It is at this point in the book that the aim of searching deep within to find evidence of the transcendent source is explained. In this regard, the whole of Freemasonry is revealed as having the same ultimate aim as every other tradition that has had initiation at its core.

The total journey, as it is laid out in the book, has a spiritual as well as moral thread running all the way through, so the conclusions drawn in the final chapter will, more than likely, come as no real surprise. However, it must be understood that the journey of Freemasonry is not merely taken to be made up of just the three initiation ceremonies. It is intended that the journey of the Freemason is, in actual fact, the journey through life. After all, the lessons of the initiation ceremonies can only be tested in the laboratory of the Freemason's own life. Nothing in Freemasonry is to be taken at face value; the fact that the entire system is made up of symbolism and allegory should confirm this. Everything in the Craft is open to interpretation, and it can even be rightly said that Freemasonry is slightly different for each Freemason.

Throughout the discussion in this book, great care has been taken to ensure that the content of the Masonic ritual isn't revealed. In the final chapter, some of the ceremony of the Royal Arch is discussed, but a degree of care has also been taken here so as not to reveal too much and to spoil the experience for those who might wish to undergo that particular ceremony in the course of their Masonic career.

It has always been a tradition of Freemasonry not to talk too much about any of its ceremonies. This has given rise to some of the conspiracy theories that have arisen about Freemasonry.

The main myth is that the Freemasonry must be a secret society. It is not. If Freemasonry were a secret society, you would not be reading this book, as it would have been forbidden to be written and published. Equally, no one would know anyone who was prepared to admit to being a Freemason. Yet there are many, such as myself, who proudly acknowledge their membership to anyone who is interested in talking about it.

There is nothing overtly secret about any of the ceremonies in Freemasonry, and all Freemasons are free to talk about them if they so wish. However, they generally refuse to do so because to reveal too much about the actual experience of Masonic initiation would pre-empt what a person who is interested in joining might encounter when they do join. This would most certainly rob them of the value of going through initiation without knowing what is coming.

However, it cannot be said that there are no secrets in Freemasonry. The methods of recognition that are used between Masons are kept secret. These comprise the infamous handshakes and passwords. However, despite yet more conspiracy theories to the contrary, these methods of recognition are only to be used within the context of Freemasonry itself. To ensure that the details of Masonic initiation are kept within the confines of those who understand the value of not talking about it (in other words, existing Freemasons) the methods of recognition are kept secret so that no one who is not really a Freemason can enter a lodge meeting and gain access to viewing an initiation.

It might be important to disclose at this point that there are no grisly outcomes awaiting a Freemason who speaks about the secrets in Freemasonry. It is extremely likely however that their resignation from the Order would be requested. It is expected that a Freemason will keep the necessary secrets on their honour.

In many ways, the preservation as a mystery to the non-Masonic world of the details of initiation is carrying on the traditions of such systems. In the ancient past, no person could know the details of any of the organisations that were, at the time, called the Mysteries. Only those who were members would have access to such information.

With all this in mind, this book is limited to discussing only those symbols that serve its central thesis of the progress in Freemasonry being seen as a journey in stone.

CHAPTER 1

WHAT IS FREEMASONRY?

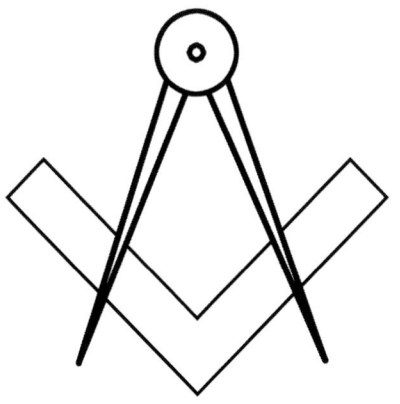

'The square and compasses of Freemasonry.'

Freemasonry defines itself as 'a peculiar system of morality, veiled in allegory and illustrated by symbols.' However, if it is a system of morality, why would such a system need to be hidden behind allegory and symbolic language? Wouldn't it be better to express this morality in very plain terms so that everyone would be clear about what was being said? To answer these questions we need to understand how Freemasonry was derived from a far more ancient tradition.

Since ancient times, humanity has always felt that there is a deeper truth underlying what we experience in the everyday world. The big questions have always been asked, and none of these questions come bigger than: 'how is it that there is something rather than nothing?' Human beings seem to have always been preoccupied with the question of existence and how everything came to be. We have always felt, deep down inside, if we really examine our feelings, that there is some truth out there. We may not know what this truth looks like, but we seem to know that it is there. Indeed, it is the sense that there is a fundamental truth of existence just beyond our grasp that has driven the development of religion, philosophy and science. Throughout history we have been driven to seek answers.

We have looked for the answers in two places: the world around us, and the world within. The study of phenomena around us is the realm of science and rationalism. With science and logic we can observe the events happening around us, and understand causes and effects. However, no matter how much of the physical universe we observe and understand, we have not quite been able to find answers that satisfy the something that we feel deep inside. We might be able to describe the world around us with language and mathematics: when ordinary language can't quite grasp some of the realities beyond our senses, mathematics becomes the dominant descriptive language. There is a point, though, where both ordinary language and mathematics become unable to describe how the universe came into being. It seems that science can only take us so far. We might be able to understand everything in the world around us, perhaps even the universe around us, all the way back to the first units of time after the Big Bang, but beyond this point science fails. Nothing seems to be able to answer the question of why there is something rather than nothing at all. If science and language fail to describe how the universe comes into being, they also fail to explain how the material universe maintains its existence at the most fundamental level.

The other way of finding the answer to this most fundamental of questions is by looking within instead of without. Since human beings have always felt deep down that there is a truth about our existence, techniques have been developed that allow individuals to dig down within our unique human experiences to find what we seem to know lies at the very centre of our being. We have mentioned that this ultimate reality cannot be described or communicated; it can only be apprehended through practised tuning of the mind and emotions. One major technique for helping a person to mine human experience to dig towards the truth is called initiation.

Initiation is a process that requires a human being to progress through a symbolic journey that alters their perspective in some deep and fundamental way. It usually requires the Candidate for initiation to be encouraged to leave their usual rational senses behind and look at the world using their deeper senses. Therefore, the journey of initiation is one that cannot be understood in a literal way. The symbols that an Initiate encounters in an initiation ceremony are usually presented with little description, causing the mind of the individual to seek the meanings for the symbols for themselves. The word 'initiation' means to begin, and the Initiate, having begun their quest, embarks on a life of study of the inner world and how that world relates to the outer reality.

The ultimate aim of this inner quest is to uncover the truth at the heart of all existence, following the sense that it somehow seems to reside deep down within us like a spring. As we are material parts of the universe who happen to have consciousness that enables us to sense something deep down, the natural conclusion is that the truth at our core is the same truth which is to be found at the core of the inanimate. The Initiate might feel that if they follow the river of inner experience to its source they will come into a direct knowledge of the secret behind all things. However, the nature of this ultimate secret is such that, as we have discussed, it cannot be described or communicated. If the neophyte discovers this elusive secret at all, it will forever remain a secret to the outside world, as the seeker lacks the capability to communicate it. They would have sense of it, and would be able to understand it at the instinctive level, but that is where it will always remain. Naturally, the new discovery might alter the behaviour of the individual in some way, but this is the only clue that anyone would glean that a discovery had been made. An illustration of this that most people will be able to understand is the experience of love. We all know what it feels like to love something or someone, but we can never adequately describe what that emotion feels like to us. Others might see us behave in a way that they have learned is associated with love, and would conclude that we do indeed love the object or person of our focus. However, these observed behaviours in no way communicate to them what our love feels like to us. They might be able to match these behaviours to the feeling of love they experience, but they can never be sure if the feeling they call love feels the same as the feeling we call love. The same is true of everything else in the realm of emotions. For this reason, the initiation process is a deeply personal experience.

In ancient Greek times the temple of the oracle at Delphi had, inscribed above the door, the famous phrase 'Know thyself.' This simple command is linked to the idea of initiation, because the whole process of looking within is a process of self-discovery. We all come into this world a complete stranger to ourselves, and we only discover ourselves as we live our lives. Bearing this in mind, a ceremony of initiation could easily be seen as representing an individual's journey through life. Indeed, the process of initiation in Freemasonry is split emblematically into three parts to represent the three main phases of existence: birth, the journey of life, and death. The initiation itself then allows the Candidate to view life as a journey that slowly reveals who they are. The old phrase 'what doesn't kill us makes us stronger' is another way of expressing this process. As life naturally throws challenges at us, we sometimes need to look within for resources to deal with the problems at hand. When the problems are solved, we come out the other side a different person: we have learned a little more about who we are, and what we are capable of. Many people even purposefully take on new challenges because of their understanding of this fact. They wonder how far they can stretch themselves and how much more they can learn about themselves. The daily living of life then allows us to unfold our natures. In a Masonic way of looking at things, it is almost as if life chisels away at us, revealing our inner selves chip by chip.

It is no coincidence that I have mentioned the metaphor of self-development as if a person is a stone being chiselled to reveal something more. This is exactly the metaphor that is used in Freemasonry. Using the tools that a stonemason would use to produce building-blocks for a building, Freemasonry has created a framework of symbols for the purposes of initiation. Whereas ordinary operative stone-masonry is all about the working of stone for particular purposes, Freemasonry is all about working on the Self throughout one's life to refine oneself to discover the deeper person within. However, we have said that Freemasonry is a tradition of initiation, so how does morality come into all of this?

Morality is about how we live our lives, and what examples we set. It defines how we relate to others in the various aspects of our lives. It includes rules about keeping in due bounds with the law, but it also governs how we conduct our lives generally, such as ensuring we keep a promise for example.

Freemasonry concerns itself with morality because of its origins in the stone-guilds. The techniques of stone-masonry were much sought-after secrets, and to ensure that they weren't transmitted outside of the guild it was important to ensure that members of a stonemasons' lodge were men of honour who could be trusted to keep the trade-secrets to themselves. The initiation rituals of masonry were designed so that a Candidate would learn and keep in mind the expectation that they were to remain honourable and trustworthy. As the power of the stone-guilds died away, and honorary 'free and accepted' members became the dominant membership, the rituals were made to apply to life in general.

Morality has traditionally been seen as being taught by parents, teachers, and institutions such as religions. However, the initiation rituals of Freemasonry give a fresh perspective from the point of view of discovery. Candidates who are led through Masonic initiations discover, on their journey, the symbols that are meant to reflect aspects of morality. Since these objects are only symbols, the inquisitive mind is led down the path of further study in an endeavour to understand the meaning of the symbolism; as a result, a profound moral change in the individual is hopefully produced. Rather than being told how to be moral, the Masonic Candidate has crafted themselves and discovered a new moral Self within who has achieved an intimate understanding of the reason behind morality. This is why the 'peculiar system of morality' of Freemasonry is 'veiled in allegory and illustrated by symbols.'

The lessons of Freemasonry reach far further than moral conduct however. A good set of morals often alludes to acts of selflessness, and this has far deeper implications than the understood benefit to the people around us. We have already seen that initiation allows Candidates to dig down into themselves in a quest to discover the hidden secrets of life and the world. It has already been argued that the truth that the Initiate seeks is indescribable in ordinary language, and can only be found using internal processes. As a person goes through life seeking a unifying truth, it is important that they focus on the interconnectedness of the wider world. To this end, selfless thought and action draws the attention away from the Self and towards others. It is hoped that continued selfless action will diminish the importance of the Self and help an individual to discern the subtle underlying connections in the world of which we are all merely a part.

Morality can be construed as thinking of others and our individual connection to others, and so a system of morality, as well as serving as a way to improve general social relations, also has the advantage of helping us discover the hidden secrets of ourselves and the world.

One of the most obvious ways that Freemasonry encourages selfless thought and action amongst its members is through charity. Freemasonry gives to many charities around the world, and its ceremonies teach Initiates to act charitably in their lives, charity being the distinguishing characteristic of a Freemason's heart.

Having a framework of morality also allows people to challenge themselves. If a situation occurs where a problem must be solved but moral rules must also be followed, it forces us to be creative so that the problems of life can be solved yet our moral codes upheld at the same

'Venturing into the dark to find the source.'

time. By having a moral code we present ourselves with obstacles to circumvent. Once we have solved each problem, with morality unscathed, we come out the other side having learned and having grown. Using the analogy of crafting ourselves, the self-imposed obstacles of our own morality help us to chip away at the very material of ourselves to reveal more of our potential.

The human brain can only understand new concepts in terms of things that it already understands, so symbols, which are rich in metaphor, can help a person to engage with subjects of which they have little previous experience. An example of a symbol could be the image of a river flowing out of a cave. On the surface, all we have is a cave with water flowing out of it. Questions might arise here, however, such as where the river is flowing from. To answer this question we should imagine travelling up the river into the darkness of the cave. As the darkness closes around us, we might become fearful and start to think that perhaps we should turn round and return to the safety of the light outside. After all, we are trying to move upstream, against the flow of the river, and it would be very easy to just let the current carry us back out to safety. If we continue on, however, we find that we come to a spring that seems to well up from the ground. It might become obvious that this is not just a story about finding the source of a river. The cave might represent the Self for instance. The journey into the dark cave could represent a search through the levels of deeper psychology, and the discovery of the spring might represent a unifying core of being that is awaiting discovery within. This is the power of symbolism and allegory. We are hard-wired to be able to represent new things in terms of things we have seen before, i.e. things that might act similarly. When a person thinks in this way, the whole of life becomes a rich canvas of symbolism. To the Initiate, the workings of the world around them can provide some hint of a deeper meaning, so long as they ensure that they attend to the meaning of the symbols that lie all around.

A famous allegory is that of Plato's cave. Plato was an ancient Greek philosopher who was the student of Socrates. In his cave allegory three men are chained inside a cave, having spent their entire lives there, staring at the back wall, with their backs to the entrance. As the sun shone through the entrance, shadows of passers-by would be cast onto the back wall, and the three in the cave interpreted this as the whole of reality. At one point, one of the three is released and ventures outside. At first the sun hurts his eyes, but when he adjusts to his new surroundings he sees the true reality in all its glory. On returning to the inside of the cave he tries to convince the others of the true reality he has witnessed, but they fail to believe him. This story provided rich symbolism for Plato's audiences. With it he meant to convey that the world around us was like a world of shadows that were projected from the real world of perfect forms that he theorised to exist. He maintained that the philosopher was like the man who left the cave who, having discovered the truth behind all things, had a duty to inform his former companions, and try his best to convince them. The idea that this world is some imperfect representation of a richer world behind the scenes is clearly illustrated in this allegory.

For the stonemasons of the past, their working practices and tools provided a rich source of symbolism. As they learned the use of each of the tools and techniques it was a small leap to devise how they might provide metaphors for deeper insights into morality. The crafting of a stone is a perfect metaphor for the crafting of the Self. Everything that was familiar to the worker of stone could help them to truly assimilate the meanings of deeper concepts if they attended to their meanings. As well as symbols, an allegory was devised to link the symbolism together, which provided the basis for the initiation that a Masonic Candidate would journey through. As the Initiate saw the everyday tools with which they were already familiar presented to them in the context of a morality story, they would instantly be able to see how the objects were trying to describe something deeper. Later, as the stonemason used these everyday tools, techniques, and objects in their day-to-day work, they would have a constant reminder of the deeper moral lessons that had been presented to them in their initiation.

For modern Freemasons, who mostly do not work stone at all, the same symbols are presented to them using allegory and story-telling, in which the Candidate experiences themselves as the main protagonist. Although some of the objects from the tradition of operative masonry may be unfamiliar to the modern Masonic Initiate, enough meaning is provided so that they might later ponder how the concepts and tools of stonework might be similar to moral ideas in a metaphorical way. The symbols provide a vivid illustration, and, as in all initiation traditions of the past, once the Candidate becomes used to thinking in a symbolic way they can begin to see symbols all around them, perhaps alluding to some deeper truth lying just beyond the grasp of the ordinary senses.

Of course, in order for initiation to have the powerful impact it is intended to have, the Candidate must be properly prepared so that they may get the full benefit of the experience. Being properly prepared means that the Candidate's mind needs to be put into a receptive state. One of the best ways of doing this is to ensure that the person due to undergo initiation feels a sense of apprehension about what it is that lies behind the closed doors through which they are about to venture. Generally speaking, when a human being feels apprehensive about an impending event, their mind becomes alert. The apprehension comes from the fact that the Candidate is about to step into the unknown. This is one of the reasons why there appears to be so much secrecy surrounding what happens in a Masonic meeting. It is largely because an initiation usually takes place during a meeting, and keeping the details of the initiation ceremonies a secret helps preserve the sense of the unknown for Candidates who wish to become members of the Order. Once the doors open, the Candidate is boldly stepping into the territory of a new experience that will have a profound effect on them. To be exact, there is no official secrecy surrounding the content of the Masonic ceremonies, but generally Freemasons refrain from talking about it so that it is not spoiled for potential Candidates.

It cannot be denied, however that there is a fair amount of rumour concerning the 'secrets' of Freemasonry. It is true that there are Masonic secrets but, despite certain conspiracy theories, they are far from sinister. Indeed, the only 'official' secrets of Freemasonry take the form of passwords and handshakes. These are kept secret because they are supposed to be official methods of recognition between members, and only members are allowed to know them so that they can prove their membership should they visit a Masonic lodge at which they are not readily known.

The handshakes themselves have often been the subject of conspiracy theories. It is sometimes thought that these handshakes are used in the everyday lives of Freemasons so that other members can distinguish them from the rest of the population for the purpose of gaining special privileges or preferential treatment. This is not what the handshakes are for. In fact, any Mason who is found to be using their membership as a way of gaining benefit in their day-to-day lives run the risk of being expelled from membership. The organisation of Freemasonry makes it very clear that being a member is not a passport to any preferential treatment.

Instead, the handshakes allow a Mason to prove that they are members of the Order, should they be tested upon entering a lodge where they are not known to the membership. There is a strong tradition of Masons visiting meetings of lodges other than their own. Since the meetings are restricted to Masons, members clearly need be able to demonstrate that they may be allowed access, and the handshakes provide this ability.

Of course, the handshakes are not necessarily secure on their own, and so they are accompanied by certain passwords known between Masons, and the passwords need to be delivered in a certain way.

The tradition of using handshakes for recognition is thought to come from the time of the mediaeval stone-guilds. It has already been mentioned that stonemasons were free to travel from one province to another to find work. When a stonemason from another area chanced upon a site where stonemasons were working, the traveller would have to prove that he was a member of the guild as well as his level of proficiency, so that he could be placed in the correct line of work and paid the necessary dues. While they worked, masons from far afield would often be given simple accommodation at the building-site. It was therefore very much the tradition of operative stonemasons, as it is for Freemasons today, for members to visit the meetings of other lodges.

It should also be explained, at this point, that Masonic meetings restrict non-members from attending because the content of the initiation ceremonies are for those who are being initiated and for those who already have been initiated. As mentioned previously, to preserve the impact of initiation, details are not widely advertised to the non-Masonic world, and so anyone who is not a member who obviously wouldn't be trusted not to spread the word is barred from attending Masonic meetings.

The association of secrets with Freemasonry is further compounded by the erroneous idea that it is a secret society. This is not the case. A secret society is literally that: secret. No one would be aware of the membership of a secret society, or of when or where they met, nor would such members reveal their membership in public. However, Masonry makes no secret of its membership. Famous celebrities, presidents, prime ministers, royals, and ordinary members of the public are on public record as being Freemasons. Lodge meetings are held in lodges that are easy to find, and any casual observer would be able to find out when the meetings took place if they wanted to. Also, Freemasons are often present, in full Masonic regalia, at various public events, such as the laying of foundation-stones at some new buildings and parades such as those commemorating the fallen in battle on Remembrance Day. Freemasons' lodges even hold open days for non-members to visit and attend talks about Freemasonry in general.

It can be seen that Freemasonry is in no way a secret society. Instead, it is a society for private members that has secrets associated with it: the aforementioned handshakes and passwords. Even the content of the meetings isn't really secret. Any Mason is free to talk about Masonic ceremonies but, for reasons already mentioned, they tend not to.

Other than the secrets already mentioned, there is another secret that is kept. However this secret is not merely the province of Freemasonry alone. It is a secret that lies within all of us, and tends to keep itself. This secret concerns our deepest natures, and it may only reveal itself after much inner seeking, aided by the process of initiation.

As a system of morality, Freemasonry also practices three main tenets: brotherly love, relief, and truth. The first of these three is all about a focus on those things that make us the same. Freemasons, within the context of Freemasonry, are united under a common symbolic framework. Freemasonry is very focused on encouraging its members to share in the plights of their brethren and to be there as a brother. This has often been misconstrued as Freemasonry being focused on mutual help based on favouritism. Again this is incorrect. As with everything in Freemasonry, the concept of brotherly love is a symbol. It is intended to represent a general love of our neighbours within wider society. It is termed brotherly love because Masonic lodges are traditionally fraternal in nature, but it is the sentiment that is the important thing here. Freemasonry highlights how every human being is subject to the same challenges in life. Regardless of how rich or poor anyone is, no matter what a person's good points or bad points are we are all threatened by potential ill-health, the shifting of the economy and, whether we like to admit it or not, by the fact that death will always take us in the end. We are all in the same boat.

However, when we look at the world today we see a society that is fragmented. There are political differences, religious differences: there are differences everywhere. Rather than concentrating on the fact that we are all human, with human problems, we fight and argue and bicker. If the people of the world began to regard each person as needing the support of every other person, the world would perhaps be a far better place to live.

The rules of conduct in a Masonic meeting state that members should refrain from having political and religious discussion. Again this is all to ensure that Freemasons do not focus on those things which divide us as people, but instead focus on that which unites. Freemasonry is open to everyone of moral character, no matter their religious background. In fact Freemasonry has a symbolic name that it uses for God, which is the 'Great Architect of the Universe.' All prayers are addressed to the Great Architect so that, no matter what religion a member follows, they will see the symbolic name as representing their faith's concept of deity. Obligations that take place are made on the 'Volume of the Sacred Law' which is a symbolic name for the main scripture of any faith. Generally, the Bible is laid open in most English lodges, featuring as the Volume of the Sacred Law, but during obligations this can be a volume that represents the central scripture of the Candidate's own faith. Once again, this is all done in a spirit of inclusion, regardless of any obvious differences, Masons are gathered together as Masons.

This means that they are gathered as people who believe in some kind of supreme being, who wish to lead mindfully moral lives, and who enjoy the philosophical challenges of Masonic ritual.

Obviously, Masons do differ in their political opinions as well but, throughout history, the restraint on talking about political topics in Masonic lodges has allowed Masons who have perhaps been on opposite sides during wartime to sit together, without quarrel, in the context of Masonry. This inclusion of people of opposing political opinions has sometimes caused suspicion from governments that there must be something secret being concocted behind the closed doors of a lodge that might pose some threat. It is for this reason that dictators like Adolf Hitler have tried to destroy Freemasonry. However, thanks to the rule of refraining from political discussion, Freemasonry can avoid any danger of such suspicions from becoming a reality.

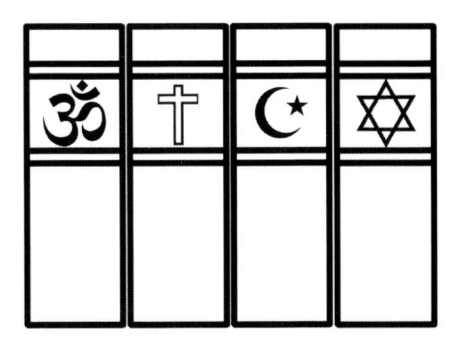

'Volumes of the Sacred Law.'

Brotherly love in Freemasonry, then, is a symbol of a sense of inclusion and mindfulness of our fellow human beings. It shouldn't be seen as being restricted to males only. As we have mentioned before, Masonry has traditionally been a fraternal system, and so the term brotherly love is an obvious one to use between members of a predominantly male organisation.

The second main tenet of Freemasonry is relief. This is all about charitable action, to provide relief to our fellow human beings in need. Freemasonry as an organisation practices the virtue of charity. It is very quick to release funds to communities in the grip of natural disasters, wherever they are in the world. Money is also donated to scientists around the world to help them in their search for the cures for the many ailments that plague humankind. It is the wish of Freemasonry as an organisation to be a source of good, and charity is one of the ways it attempts to achieve this end.

In Masonic initiations, the virtue of charity is impressed upon the Candidate so that they become intimately aware that there is a wider need for them to think in charitable terms, and to quickly spot situations where they can offer help. This does not just mean financial charity, however. We should also understand that human beings can give the gift of time as an act of charity. Helping someone when they need assistance, without the requirement of payment, can be one of the most helpful things we can do for others. It is also something everyone can do, even when they have little money.

At lodge meetings, at least one charitable collection takes place to which Masons donate money. The amount that is donated has no expectation associated with it. All charitable giving should be in such a way that the person giving is not adversely affected. No matter what value is donated to a collection by an individual, it is gratefully accepted and faithfully applied. The money collected by lodges is collected in a charitable account, so that the lodge may make donations as the need arises. There are also a few general charitable funds that have been specifically set up by Freemasonry to support particular causes, and sometimes lodge collections are used to support these.

It should be understood that, unlike charitable organisations that are widely known who have to use some funding to support staff wages and overhead costs, everything that is given in the name of charity by members of Freemasonry is applied fully to charitable causes. All other funds required by Freemasonry to support itself as an organisation are paid for in members fees.

The true virtue of charity is that it is entirely selfless in nature. Having a strong focus on charitable giving encourages a person to consider others instead of just themselves. Since the process of initiation is intended to help the Candidate to appreciate deeper and wider facets of life, the inclusion of charity is a way of enabling the Initiate to see the links of interdependency that exist between human beings. It teaches the important lesson that no human being is an island, and that every individual depends on the actions of others. This charitable giving, when practised regularly, should then set an example to others.

Giving has the effect of making those who give feel good that they have improved the life or happiness of someone else. The feeling a person can gain from believing that they have helped another person is priceless, and it is this feeling, when regularly felt, that serves to give a human being a sense of some true purpose. Often, feeling good about an action is a sure way to sense that the action was the right thing to do, and so if helping others generates good feelings then this must mean that helping others is something we have evolved to do.

True charitable thinking also encourages an individual to think about and appreciate the plight of other people. The ability to step into someone else's shoes and empathise with what they might be feeling allows us to understand the human condition on a wider level. When we learn to appreciate the struggles of other people enough to lend our support, we get a better sense of how everyone is the same deep down, despite their seemingly obvious differences. Paradoxically, as we learn about the similarities we share with other people we can learn more about ourselves at a deeper level. We understand ourselves and other people in such a way as to foster the first tenet of brotherly love. Indeed, charitable giving is another way that brotherly love can be expressed. Working together, brotherly love and relief will encourage a necessary cohesion between human beings.

The final main tenet of Freemasonry is truth. Truth, as Freemasonry interprets it, means both the telling of the truth and the search for a deeper truth. The first meaning, that of being truthful and honest, is perhaps one of the most important characteristics for an individual living in a cohesive society. Honesty can lubricate the wheels of human relationships. When a human being has nothing to hide there comes with that feeling a certain element of peace. It is well known that if a lie is told, a fair amount of mental resources are required to ensure that the real truth doesn't come out. Then, of course, the longer the truth is kept veiled, the less the person who told the lie feels they can reveal the reality. Avoiding telling lies means that one doesn't have to worry about anything hidden suddenly being revealed.

Of course, other than perhaps in the case of the compulsive liar, a person will only lie out of fear. A liar is usually frightened that the truth will cause them some distress or to be held in lower esteem. Either that, or they fear that the truth will cause distress in another person. However, so long as the truth is delivered with diplomacy, as the situation might dictate, being honest does the very important job of overcoming this innate social fear.

If we maintain a practice of being honest and truthful then we are no longer wearing a mask that we present to the world. Instead, the face you display is your own. Everyone around you understands who you are and what you are about. Inevitably this means that those around you will be able to trust what you say and see that you have integrity, both of which are essential for harmonious human relations. Being honest also allows relationships to start on a foundation that is based entirely on truth. Regardless of how bad an item of truth may look, it is still truth, and this means true progress and growth can take place.

The policy of being truthful forces a human being to face what they fear in themselves, and reveal it for all to see. In reality, this is the only way that we can truly see what our place is in the world. If we show a lie to the world, the world will engage with a fictitious character and little benefit will come, but if we show our true selves, the world will interact with reality, and meaningful change will take place for both the world, other people, and the individual themselves.

The other way of looking at truth is in the context of the search for truth. This is, of course, talking about discovering what reality is: it is the search for knowledge. In order to facilitate this interpretation of the last main tenet, Freemasonry encourages the study of the seven liberal arts and sciences. These are: logic, arithmetic, geometry, grammar, rhetoric, music, and astronomy. The seven liberal arts and sciences are a tradition of study stretching from ancient times, and are seen as the most important subjects for the shaping of the mind. They encourage a general understanding of the material universe. Logic is the innate capacity of a human being to discover relationships between elements of the world. A notion of logic is that if A is equal to B and B is equal to C, then A must be equal to C. This particular relationship between three values appears to be innate and to exist separately from the human mind. The further relationships of logical reasoning also appear to exist independently. It would seem that logic is written into the very fabric of the universe.

Moving from logic, we have arithmetic, which is the human language that expresses the innate logic discovered in the universe. Mathematics allows us to represent the material world in a type of language where the grammar is logic. With mathematics we can predict how the world is likely to be, then devise experiments to see if the reality matches the prediction.

Geometry is a particular application of arithmetic, mainly concerned with the relationships and distances between objects in the world. With geometry, we can model how the world looks, and we can understand how the forces that intervene between these objects operate. Many equations in physics are based on the mathematical science of geometry.

Leaving the realm of logic, we come to language, beginning with grammar. Grammar, of course, is the structuring of words in a way so that we can effectively communicate. Related to grammar is rhetoric. Rhetoric is the art of persuasion, and is the science of how to put together a convincing argument. In essence, rhetoric is the art of effective communication supported by the structuring of well-executed grammar.

The study of music is the study of the relationship between sounds. We know that certain combinations of sounds can create lovely harmonies. We also know that the combination of other sounds create cacophonies. The study of music then is the understanding of the relationships between sounds to create pieces that influence the mind and soul. In a way, music could be seen as a kind of grammar, and a form of rhetoric.

The final science is that of astronomy, or the study of the wider universe, and how celestial bodies move and are held together to structure the wider reality of what exists. By understanding the wider universe, we can understand aspects of our own corner of the universe and, perhaps eventually, understand how it all works and how it came into being. The observations of astronomy are also reliant on the aforementioned logic, arithmetic, and geometry.

In the liberal arts and sciences, then, we have a ladder of understanding. From the foundation-rungs of the mathematical, progressing to the fundamentals of language and thought, through the science of influencing the soul, we are led to the top rung of how all this is placed in the wider universe. This is why these particular subjects are considered essential in preparing the mind for greater understanding.

The realms of seeking knowledge are not just restricted to the liberal arts and sciences of course. Acquiring any aspect of knowledge of the wider world is a way of understanding truth. If we understand psychology, for instance, we can try to learn why humans behave the way they do, while biology helps us understand how chemistry underpins life, and this helps us to develop effective medicines.

However, none of these elements of study is likely to reveal a complete picture of the world unless it includes the truth of the Self. Understanding the truth of the Self is the reason for initiation and also ties into the aspect of truth associated with honesty. Only when you are expressing your truthful Self and are, at the same time, moving towards understanding the truths of the material universe will a complete picture start to become visible.

A Mason, then, is a seeker of truth, both in themselves and the world in which they live. They are a person who, in seeing the plight of others, sees purpose in reaching out in aid, and attempts to illuminate the truth of interdependency. Finally, they are a person who seeks to see others on equal terms and understands that the only thing that matters, despite obvious differences, is the fact that we are part of the same human family. The peculiar system of morality, veiled in allegory and illustrated by symbols, provides a framework of philosophy against which Freemasons can measure and hopefully navigate their lives

Having a unifying philosophy in life has been important to mankind throughout its history. Such a philosophy can help to guide a person on how to live their life.

When we first come into this life and start to be able to make sense of world around us we would find ourselves lost if we didn't have a framework within which to live. The first framework of behaviour we perceive in the world is given to us by our parents, and this provides a foundation for the rest of our lives. As children, we watch how our parents react to particular situations. We then tend to follow their behaviour when we see those situations happen to us.

Beyond our parents, once we begin to acquire friends and as we liaise with our peers we learn how they think, feel, and react. At this stage our framework for life, or unifying philosophy, expands and adapts as we hopefully become better social creatures.

As well as our friends and acquaintances, we have what is received from stories in books, films, and television. There is also the influence of belief-systems like religions that can have a powerful and fundamental influence on our moralistic behaviour. Eventually, we develop a unifying philosophy to which we can refer in order to carry ourselves through the different challenges in life.

As a philosophical framework, Freemasonry is another source in which moral standards can be found. However, as we have already seen, it is a philosophy that includes an element of introspection, with a view to helping the individual to understand who they are, for the benefit of those around them. It is a philosophy that tries to inculcate a total understanding of life and individual purpose.

By using symbols, Freemasonry encourages the Initiate to think symbolically, and to understand the world in such terms and perhaps uncover a deeper meaning to things.

As a Freemason progresses they can use life to discover who they are by solving the problems and challenges as they meet them on the way, using their experiences in life to help them grow, or to sculpt them, in Masonic terms.

As they slowly carve away at themselves to reveal who they are deep down, the Mason can discover new aspects of themselves that they didn't even necessarily know were there. The Mason can then express these new-found qualities as we move through life, for the benefit of others and themselves. They can find deeper purpose and happiness as they start to feel that they are performing meaningful acts that are a true and honest reflection of the person they are slowly discovering.

In relationships, the Mason may discover that they can give more and be more selfless, in the understanding that we are all interdependent and that giving is the best use of a human being's time and the best way of finding purpose. Furthermore, from developing an understanding of the processes of change and that people are never static in life a Mason can learn to accommodate that change and grow alongside those whom they wish to have in their lives. When things get rough in relationships, it is often best to have the honesty to accept that the other person is not always entirely to blame, and that the rough times are ideal times for self-development.

I hope that this chapter has outlined what Freemasonry is all about but, to understand further how the symbolic tradition of Freemasonry can help a person to grow, we must look more closely at the particular symbolism of the Society. Specifically, we must look at the most fundamental aspect of Freemasonry: the stone that represents the individual on its journey from the symbolic quarry to the symbolic edifice for which it is meant. We must look at how this stone is worked upon and honed to render it more useful by following it on its journey of being worked upon by the symbolic tools of Freemasonry. In the end, we will see how some basic symbolism transforms a Masonic Candidate from who they were into someone new. Eventually it will be shown how the potential that has lain, perhaps untapped, within a person can be revealed for the benefit of society at large and the individual themselves.

The best place to start, then, is at the beginning, with the individual Candidate before they embark upon their journey in stone.

CHAPTER 2

THE ROUGH ASHLAR

'The Rough Ashlar.'

When Michelangelo began working on his statue of David it is said that he spent a lot of time just sitting there, looking at the huge block of marble. One day his commissioners spotted him apparently idling, and went up to him to ask him why he didn't seem to be doing any work. Michelangelo replied that he *was* working. He was imagining the form of the statue within the marble block so that he knew which parts he needed to chip away.

This story tells us something about the symbolism of the rough ashlar, namely that it represents the Masonic Candidate before he goes through the first stage of his initiation, and that he is like a stone taken fresh from the quarry within which there is an ideal form waiting to be revealed. Freemasonry, then, is the work that is done on the rough ashlar to bring out the new form.

The new form within represents the individual's potential to be something more than what he is. Society relies on its individual members, and the more each person can do to benefit that society, the more that society will benefit as a whole. However, this hidden potential is buried away, deep inside. It is hidden even from the individuals themselves. Generally speaking, human beings grow up with the idea that they must get a job in order to earn money, in order to have a decent life. The better educated a person is, the better job they can have. Whilst this is true, perhaps the focus of the individual needs to shift. Instead of learning things that will aid the pursuit of money, perhaps a better way of looking at everything is for a person to look within and understand what talents they have. Then the focus would be to develop these inner talents in order to see how they can be directed to serve society in the best way possible.

No one gives us an instruction booklet when we enter this world, and we are all finding our way in the dark, taking our cues of how to live life from those around us. The thing is, those people around us are doing exactly the same thing that we are. The rough ashlar represents the person who has lived life so far in this normal way, and has perhaps given very little thought as to the potential that really lies inside.

Finding talents that lie within and developing them is a far better way of leading a more fulfilling life. All work that is performed from this point of view becomes an extension of the person. Rather than being viewed as 'work', the person finds that they are doing what they love to do. This feeling of doing what they love allows the person to be happy in their jobs. A person utilising the talents they know they have makes every job full of purpose.

Freemasonry can take the raw material in a person and, as the meaning of the symbolism in Freemasonry begins to do its work, the person can slowly uncover who they really are and what they are capable of doing.

Furthermore, as we have seen, many cultures throughout the ages have believed that there is something deeper to reality than can be uncovered and understood at the personal level. This deeper essence answers the question 'why is it that there is something rather than nothing?' Being a part of the material universe, it makes sense that a human being also shares this essence as the ground of their being. A human being also has the capacity to be conscious and self-aware. This puts us into a unique position to detect this essence. Detecting this essence, though, requires effort and industry. It requires us to be able to dig down into ourselves and chip away until the inner reality is revealed. After concerted effort, the Freemason may come to an understanding of where this essence lies within themselves.

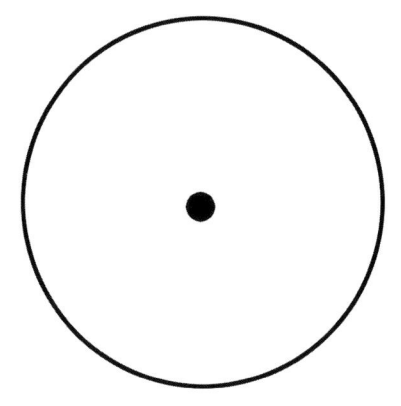

'The point within a circle, denoting the inner Self.'

Potentially, this can be very productive. Feeling this 'centre' of being can help us navigate life with an element of understanding. Being aware of this essence can help us understand the world around us in a personal way. We can utilise this faculty to gather innate understanding. This is the true meaning of the term 'wisdom.'

Thousands of years ago, a system of thought was developed in China called Taoism. This maintained that there exists a principle known only as the Tao or 'way' in which everything has its being. It taught that bringing one's life into line with this 'way' enables the Taoist to live from a place of wisdom. In the Taoist tradition, wisdom is not something that can be compared to ordinary knowledge. Nor can it be considered a kind of knowledge paired with experience of life. Instead, wisdom was seen as like a flowing river that one could dip into and utilise, but which could never be captured. A practised Taoist could live from the centre of all things where the spring of wisdom resides, psychologically immersing themselves in it to aid them with the problems of life.

The idea that the source of wisdom is an elusive underlying force that cannot be apprehended but only used is not restricted to ancient China. Hermetic philosophy, which is believed to have arisen in ancient Egypt, held that the whole of existence has its being in a universal mind. It also maintained that there is a macrocosm, i.e. the wider universe, and a microcosm, the human being. Everything that existed was in the mind of the 'All', but the 'All' was also in all. This was the way in which they understood the immanence of the ground of all being. To understand the All, the human being could delve within their own mind in order to find it. Again, wisdom could be gained from this All, once found.

Gaining insight and wisdom from delving deep within is the point of initiation, and this is no different in Masonic initiation. The difference is that the symbolism of carving stone to reveal what is within is used as a perfect metaphor for this purpose. A life lived with wisdom is one that is lived with understanding and of useful service to others. The irregularity of the rough ashlar demonstrates that there are many things that must be 'chipped away' before the deeper wisdom can be approached.

Service to others should ideally be the focus of a person entering Freemasonry. To this end, a person should already give evidence of the necessary faculties expected in a Freemason.

In building and stonework, the blocks of stone that were selected from the quarry to be worked on had to be of the best quality available. This means that they had to contain no essential faults, like cracks and weak spots. This is obvious, because if a building was indeed to be made out of such blocks, there would be no way to ensure that the structure would be stable. The selection of the block from the quarry is the symbolism of the selection of the Candidate.

Before a Candidate enters Freemasonry, it is important that certain qualifications have been met. The first qualification is that they believe in some sort of supreme being. As we have previously mentioned, it doesn't matter what sort of supreme being is believed in, so long as the Candidate believes in something greater than themselves. This is because of the tradition of initiation that is associated with Freemasonry, that is to help reveal the nature of that force within the Initiate's life. It is unlikely that a Candidate who doesn't have any belief in a supreme being will appreciate the process in its fullest sense. Also in Freemasonry, there is reference to biblical stories, along with prayers to God, therefore if an atheist joined Masonry this would appear as an irrelevant aspect and none of the story of Masonic initiation would necessarily make sense.

Another qualification expected of the Candidate is that they should have no past criminal record. If a Candidate did have a criminal record then this might mean that the foundation of the moral character of the prospective Mason was not guaranteed to be stable. This may seem harsh because, if Freemasonry's aim is to improve a person morally, then surely it should be open to those who have made mistakes in the past? Although Freemasonry does seek to improve moral conduct, it does state that a person should first be prepared to be made a Mason 'in their heart.' This means that there should be some sense of strong morality in place for Freemasonry to work on. Freemasonry does not seek to teach morality from scratch, but is meant to develop a positive morality that is already in place.

The idea that morality is already present and ready to be honed can be seen as a raw material to be worked on. The stonemason working on a building-site does not create the stone to be worked on: instead, he selects it and crafts it. Similarly, Freemasonry does not create morality, but seeks to craft it with its symbolism.

The other qualifications that a Candidate must have to join Masonry are to be of mature age, and of sound mind. These two stipulations are only required because of the developmental nature of Freemasonry, which requires a mature attitude and an ability to mentally process the philosophies within the tradition.

More specifically, the moral character of the individual should be well known enough to recommend them for membership. This is why the Candidate must have a proposer and seconder, who are already members, who can vouch for their character. If it is known that the Candidate for Freemasonry has acted in an immoral way in the past, then they should not be recommended to join.

Once the Candidate's general moral integrity has been affirmed they are now represented as the rough ashlar, not having any cracks or faults, and then and only then can they be considered for membership. However, there is still a lot of work to be done. The rough ashlar is just a rock that has been cut from the Earth. It is still a long way from being able to be considered as a worthy building element. It is still rough in appearance, and this represents the irregular nature of the Candidate's existing morals.

Although the Candidate might believe that they are a decent and moral person, they have still, so far, been finding their way through life using a moral system that has been picked from the many sources around them. The most popular understanding of where these morals come from is religion.

There are, of course, many religions in the world, and all of them have moral behaviour at their core. In the West, most people understand what is known as the 'Golden Rule.' This is embodied in 'do unto others as you would have done unto yourself.' Christians understand this as the main commandment that Jesus gave to his followers. This simple rule is meant to provide a way of understanding how to behave with other people, through knowing how you would like to be treated. If one can assume that most people have the same general likes and dislikes, we know that whatever we wouldn't want done to us other people naturally wouldn't want to happen to them. We don't like our things stolen, so we shouldn't steal; we wouldn't like to be murdered, so we shouldn't murder; we wouldn't like to be conned out of our day's pay, so we should ensure that we pay those we employ fairly, and so on. The beauty of this rule is that it relies entirely on how we see the world, and doesn't come directly from some set of laws that we are expected to follow.

In the Buddhist tradition, there is a clear focus on compassion. Again, this is almost identical to the Golden Rule, as it is expressed in Christianity. Compassion is the ability to empathise with the plight of other people. By understanding that everyone is human, and that they have the same potential emotions as we have, we can see someone who is suffering and understand what it is they are going through, simply by remembering how we felt in similar situations. The idea is that if we use compassion to feel the feelings that another person is feeling when they suffer, it becomes a natural thing for us to feel like we should take action to help. The idea of compassion also allows people to more deeply understand the deep connection between human beings. It is hoped that, as people understand that we each suffer in the same way and become more compassionate, the world will move towards a more peaceful state.

However, the sense of compassion is something that we can all naturally feel. We don't necessarily need a religious text to help us to figure out how to feel compassion. There indeed seems to be a tendency for us to automatically understand the suffering of others. This has led evolutionary biologists towards the idea that we might have evolved to feel compassion and to behave altruistically.

It is thought that, many thousands of years ago, human beings who looked after other human beings were more likely to survive. One can imagine that, when predators were a problem for human beings, along with the threat from other tribes, it was very important for people to stay in groups for strength of numbers. We see this behaviour in animals today where animals move in groups for safety. If individuals looked out for other individuals in the group, then this would make the group much stronger than if the group was composed of individuals who looked after only themselves. Over time, those who looked after themselves and formed less cohesive groups would die out, but the stronger and more cooperative groups would survive. We would then all be descended from these cooperative descendants and therefore would have inherited the genes that promote cooperative behaviour.

As well as a biological cause for potential morality, groups that communicated moral rules to each other for the benefit of the whole group would better ensure the survival of that group. These moral rules would then be passed down from generation to generation, which ties in with the idea of the scriptural origin of morality. Information that promotes survival tends to survive in itself. This does not necessarily mean that morality is of divine origin, it merely shows that those who developed rules that benefited survival would survive long enough to pass on these tips and tricks for future generations to follow in order to help them survive. As a side effect of this, the faculty of communication is slowly evolving, and so the human beings who survive turn out to be those who have the ability to tell effective moral-based stories.

It is widely known that storytelling developed to help communicate ideas about how the world worked and how a person should behave in the world. Stories are now seen as a way of entertaining ourselves, but most of us understand that most stories have a moral import or some deeper message to communicate. It would seem that this was always understood to be the most effective method of conveying information from generation to generation. The telling of stories in ancient tribes would usually be the job of the wise man or woman, who was also charged with the spiritual and physical health of the group. Naturally, this storytelling would then become the religion of a culture. The techniques of storytelling were also used in the initiation traditions of these cultures and, as we have seen in the previous chapter, these traditions of initiation were passed down over thousands of years, even inspiring Freemasonry and other traditions like it over the years.

No matter where the moral codes come from, it would appear that the leading of an ordinary modern life means that it is possible to adjust this moral system depending on the situation. This is what is meant by the irregularity of a person's morals. They are irregular because they are open to change and adaptation to suit selfish needs and desires. A more regular level of morality is necessary, so that life can be lived without compromising the rules that lead to a more harmonious society.

Every person in the world can see that we are surrounded by selfishness. The pursuit of modern life has us striving to achieve things that society tells us are worthy pursuits. A simple look at the range of advertisements presented to us on the television and the covers of magazines tells us that modern society prizes selfish pursuits. We are encouraged to strive for the big house, the nice car, the luxury holidays, for fame and for fortune. The individual human response to this suggested aim is to turn the mind to questions of how they can get these things. The focus is on the Self.

This selfish focus is what we have all grown up with. We all have an idea of 'the good life', some sense of ideal living that will make us feel free and able to do whatever we want. However, this is not quite the reality. The pursuit of this ideal has us trading our time for the finances we need to achieve these lofty aims. If saving will take too long then we are tempted to take out loans to buy the things we desire, only to be trapped in a cycle of repayments, reducing our disposable income and keeping us in work. The pursuit of the freedom advertised to us is making us quite the opposite of free.

One of the most obvious indicators of society's obsession with the Self is the modern phenomenon of the social-networking site. These sites are resplendent with communities obsessed with the idea of self-promotion, where every experience can be quickly photographed and uploaded for the rest of the world to see. Simply walking into a restaurant and looking around will allow you to see people on their phones, tagging themselves at their current locations. It would seem that there is an attitude of 'if you can't read about it on a social networking site then it didn't really happen.' These social-networking sites should have the subtitle, 'Look at me!'

In such a world of selfish pursuit a sense of morality can, to a greater or lesser extent, be very fluid in the sense that it can be adjusted to suit one's aims. It might mean that every person may have a price, and some may find themselves doing anything so long as the rewards are sufficient.

Freemasonry turns thoughts away from the pursuit of these external markers of apparent success and sets a person looking in a different direction: how they can best utilise themselves to serve others. As it turns out, if a person focuses on the service of others for its own end they tend to perform well in that particular job. Rewards usually then come in abundance if people perceive that a job is done well.

The rough ashlar doesn't just represent an irregular morality, it also represents the individual with untamed emotions. Feelings that are out of our control tend to have a direct effect on how we interact with others around us. Sometimes we can be very sensitive if people press the right buttons. We can see this by just turning on the news and seeing all the battles and unrest that seem to be perpetually occurring. Nothing seems to have changed; ever since human beings have been in existence, it would seem we are quarrelling with our neighbours. Usually, the international tensions are due to complex reasons but most of the time, it comes down to a difference of opinion, or an expression of greed. All human violence that we see is a result of our uncontrolled base emotions that have been handed down to us from our earliest history.

These bursts of negative emotion are often instant and engaged in without thinking. In order to get around this, we need to have a better sense of what is going on inside our own minds, so that we can see negative emotions rising, but stop them becoming known to the outside world. If we cease to react to our instinctive emotions, but instead control them and try to understand why we are feeling that way, we can have a more considered approach. Slowly, this will allow us to understand ourselves and our motivations.

Once we know why we react in certain ways, we can commit to changing our reactions so that there are fewer negative consequences for ourselves and others. Furthermore, by learning how and why we feel the way we do in certain situations we can develop a better understanding of other people and why they might feel the way that they do in similar situations. This then leads to being more forgiving of those around us.

The idea of looking inward to understand why we react in particular ways gives us the ability to know ourselves. It sometimes doesn't occur to people that there are reasons why they react in certain ways. Everything we do is a product of the past experiences we have had. As we move through life we often have an unacknowledged sense of insecurity, and we automatically tend to develop mechanisms that help us build walls around these inherent weak spots.

A person might, for instance, develop the characteristic where they like to be right about things. The accumulation of knowledge might be very important to them, so much so that they begin to base their entire sense of self-worth on being 'the one who knows the answers.' This person will do everything they can to prove themselves right (and therefore useful) to others. There are downsides to this, however. When a person like this is proven wrong, it can cause them to have issues with self-doubt because they have tied a sense of who they are to the ability to have knowledge about things. This means that the ego will try to prove it is right, even if that person has little knowledge about the particular topic at hand. When the person is absolutely proved wrong about something, their ego or sense of Self feels damaged, but only because they have invented a sense of who they are out of the concept of the accumulation of knowledge.

We have all met people like this, and we may even find that this, in some way, describes ourselves. These people take many forms, such as the person who has built their self-image around being good at sport, or business, or cooking, or whatever it may be. An artificial sense of Self that is tied too closely to the things that we present to the world can be too prone to damage.

To avoid this, the Masonic Candidate must learn to delve into themselves and, in the process of understanding what talents they possess and how they can express them, understand that this does not define 'who they are.' The identity of the Self is a very mysterious thing and cannot easily be pinned down. As long as the individual can disassociate themselves from those things they are good at then they will develop a deeper sense of confidence that is innate, despite how people see them.

When a Candidate first enters Freemasonry then they are entering a way of life that involves the mindful crafting of oneself. They will find that the journey on which they have embarked is broken down into three constituent parts or Degrees. Each one of these parts has particular symbols associated with them. The symbols we will mainly be interested in are what are known as the working-tools. These tools were traditionally used in the working of stone, but each one has a particular meaning that enables it to be understood in terms of its use in crafting the Self. By passing through these tools, the rough ashlar of the Candidate for initiation slowly becomes the perfect ashlar of the Master Mason.

CHAPTER 3

THE WORKING-TOOLS OF THE FIRST DEGREE

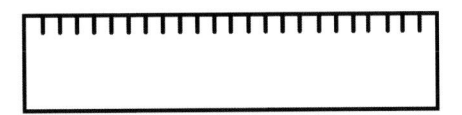

'The 24-Inch Gauge'

The First Degree in Freemasonry is called the Entered Apprentice Degree. This is the Candidate's first experience of the Masonic tradition of initiation and is designed to introduce the Initiate to the life of a Mason. When beginning their Masonic career, the Candidate has no idea what awaits them through the closed doors ahead of them. When they are admitted through the lodge doors for the first time, they are beginning a new chapter of their life.

Initiation literally means beginning. The way of life the Candidate has passed through before is coming to a close, and a new way is about to begin. The majority of Freemasonry does not take place in the lodge room; instead, its teachings are meant to be carried over by the Candidate into their ordinary life, so that they can live out in practice the principles they are introduced to. It is hoped that, as the Freemason practices the principles in life, they will slowly become conscious of their true meaning.

As part of the First Degree initiation ceremony, the Candidate will be presented with the working-tools of that Degree. There are three tools in total in this Degree, namely the twenty-four inch gauge, the common gavel, and the chisel. As with the other working-tools in the other Degrees, these tools are commonly used in actual stone working, but they are meant to have a symbolic meaning.

The first of these tools, the twenty-four inch gauge, is essentially a straight edge that enables the stonemason to measure lengths and draw lines for cutting. It is specifically twenty-four inches in length because it is meant to represent the twenty-four hours of the day. Symbolically it is meant to represent time well spent.

As human beings, we all have a limited time on Earth. It is important, therefore, that we make the most of this time. From a selfish point of view, this might be taken to mean that we should cram in as much experience as possible before we die. However, this is not the entire message taught by the gauge. The experiences of life are an important part of enjoying life, but true happiness comes from living a balanced life.

Living a balanced life means taking care of your mental, spiritual, and physical needs. Therefore, the twenty-four inch gauge teaches that time should be broken up into three distinct but not necessarily equal partitions. Our days should be spent sharing time between attending to our spiritual needs or meditation, our physical needs, and our need to seek a purpose through extending help to others.

The first of these, the spiritual aspect, is defined differently from person to person. No matter what the spiritual background of an individual, our spirit can be defined as that part of us that appears to be experiencing this life. It is our very seat of consciousness. This conscious awareness is our point of contact with everything. It is the ultimate receiver of the information coming through our senses, and it also experiences the thoughts going on inside our head.

All of this could be interpreted as some trick of the brain, but things don't seem to be that simple. The nature of experience is a very mysterious thing, and we can demonstrate this by some very simple exercises. One such simple exercise is to try to describe to someone what your experience of the colour red is like. You could point to all the red things around you and say 'that is red', but this is all you can do. You can have no idea if another person in the room experiences the same 'red' as you do. Other people can agree that you are pointing at a red object, but the only thing you know for certain, is that they learned to call that colour red, just as you did. They might be actually experiencing something quite different to you, but may still call it red. The question arises: what is colour?

Of course, we could answer this question by stating that each colour is a different wavelength of light energy, but this fails to explain what the actual experience of colour is.

To further drive this point home, and to look at it from a different angle, try to imagine an apple. If I was to monitor your brain whilst you were thinking this, I could identify all of the neurone-firing that is associated with this particular thought. However, I would not see the apple you are seeing in your head. Where then does the image you can see reside exactly? How do the firing neurones become the image, and where are you seeing the image itself? These questions are difficult if not impossible to answer. They do demonstrate however, the mystery of being, and this mystery is our spiritual aspect.

Spending time contemplating our spiritual aspect can generate valuable personal insights as to our connection with everything else, and can happen in various forms. For those with a particular religious faith it means attending to the duties of that individual religion, like praying, meditating, or studying scripture for deeper insights. For those with no particular religious faith, it means contemplating the spirit in your own individual way.

Attending to our spiritual needs often has beneficial effects. When most people truly contemplate the potential spiritual dimension of the Self, it can often give life more colour and context. Abraham Maslow identified a state of mind called the 'peak experience', which is defined as a moment of clarity where everything seems to make sense and a deep connectedness with everything is felt. Unfortunately, the peak experience is momentary, and the state is quickly forgotten.

Those who have reported a peak experience have claimed they felt that they momentarily had a glimpse of some knowledge, but that they can't remember what it was. They only experience the deep sense of peace that came from being in this state.

Returning to the peak experience is rare, but Maslow theorised that it could be cultivated and possibly extended into a desirable 'plateau experience.' This, then, is the aim of spiritual practice: to cultivate peak experiences so that we might hope to live from a place of deep insight, wisdom and peace.

The second of the three aspects of life symbolised by the twenty-four inch gauge is concerned with the material nature of life, which deals with labour and refreshment. To be happy, a person needs to take care of all of their physical needs. These needs require the spending of money, and this money usually comes from a job. It is important, therefore, to ensure that a percentage of one's day is spent focused on the performance of one's job.

Focusing on work and performing it well can usually help the progress of one's career. The logical thing, when attempting to acquire better reward, is to ensure that you perform your tasks in an exemplary manner. It is therefore important to make the constant improvement of your abilities at work your primary goal in your day-to-day business.

In China, the principle of Kung Fu was developed, which most people associate with the martial arts of the same name. The principle of Kung Fu actually means the perfection of a skill through continuous focused practice. The practice of martial arts does indeed require this kind of discipline in order to become a master of the art, but it is a principle that can be applied to anything since continuous practice always leads to the improvement of a skill.

The Freemason, then, is someone who takes the responsibility of a job well done seriously, but not only for remuneration. It is just as important to the Freemason to ensure that they are providing a good service for its own sake. Ensuring that other people are helped by the work that you do is central to a Freemason's ethics.

This aspect of the lessons taught by the gauge is not however restricted to labour itself. It is also meant to show that refreshment is just as important as labour. The old phrase 'all work and no play makes Jack a dull boy' is very true. A person cannot have a fulfilling life without taking part in things that they enjoy. Time should be spent relaxing, and ensuring that one is not unduly stressed by overwork. We must take time to entertain ourselves and spend time with our friends and family. Without these essential things, we have nothing in life but work, and human beings are not simply drones who spend their entire lives in pure service.

The final aspect of life to focus on, as taught by the gauge, is serving a friend or Brother in time of need. As we have already seen, service is a very important part of a Freemason's life, and they should be ready at all times to lend help where it is needed. We all need each other, and the world would be a far more harmonious place if everyone was willing to lend a helping hand when required.

It is important to point out however that the help that is given should not be to the detriment of ourselves, our family or other connections. It is not wise to sacrifice the comfort or happiness of yourself and the people closest to you when helping others. The help you give to others should always come from a place of abundance. We can only freely give something when we have enough to give. If we give everything we have to someone else then we might help them, but we harm ourselves in the process. Aid then, is only helpful if it's not harmful to the person giving or the people who are relying on them.

The twenty-four inch gauge, then, is about how we spend our time. It teaches that we should ensure that we attend to our needs and the needs of others, with the time that we have.

The second working-tool of this Degree is the common gavel. In stonework, the common gavel is a mallet that is used to knock off rough parts of the stone being worked on. If a stone is to be used in a building then it must have no obvious faults, and it must be smooth to fit with the other blocks. The gavel helps to ensure that the stone is turned into a smoother, more useful block. In Freemasonry, however, the common gavel represents conscience, which maintains control over anything unbecoming.

We all have faults. These faults are personality flaws that block us from being an ideal member of society. Sometimes these flaws are obvious, and so it is easy to monitor them and focus on reducing their effect. It is a difficult thing to admit to one's own faults, and an even more difficult task to break these habits so that they no longer occur. If we can reduce our faults, then we hone ourselves into a more useful individual.

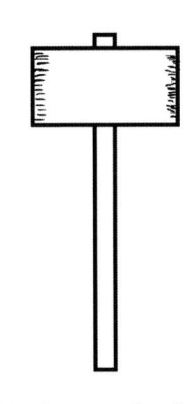

'The Common Gavel'

As they work on the stone of themselves with the common gavel, the Freemason is not only knocking away the flaws in their character, they are also getting rid of their tendency to excess.

We all indulge in excesses from time to time. Some of us indulge more times than others. These excesses can involve food, drink, or anything that we do more of in an attempt to make our lives more pleasurable and fulfilling. The problem is that if we try to derive fulfilment from external things and those things then become scarce, we lose the feeling of fulfilment they brought. This is why we have a tendency to excess. We try to have as much of everything we enjoy that we can get our hands on, because we know that these things will ultimately run out. This, of course, is the source of greed and gluttony because human beings can be tempted to try to control as much of these external things as they can, to the exclusion of others who might drain the supply more quickly.

Lasting happiness, however, should come from somewhere within. Situations can change, and we need an unchanging source of happiness for when external circumstances are not favourable. Happiness, after all, is an emotion that is generated by our brains and so, theoretically, it should be possible to invoke this state of mind at will, without relying on an external cause for it.

Maintaining a happy state of mind, however, is incredibly difficult. We pass through both the ups and the downs of life and it is hard to maintain a sense of happiness when the downsides of life occur. To cultivate a steady source of happiness we need to work hard at understanding ourselves when we are in the happy state, and understand internal triggers that can take us there whenever we want.

For a start, this means reducing our reliance on external things for happiness, so that we can be given the chance to realise that we can be happy without them. In many spiritual systems, monks renounce possessions and choose to live in poverty. To some, this may seem unnecessary: why should human beings voluntarily put themselves through austere conditions when they don't have to? Well, the answer to this is very simple: the rich tend to be very self-reliant. If they want something, they just go out and buy it, no problem. They can choose to keep themselves and their loved ones fed, clothed and sheltered. They have to look no further than their bank balance for the source of their happiness. They can rightly claim that they have made their life the way it is. However, the person who has little to no money has this apparent freedom of choice either reduced or completely taken away. No one is more sensitive to the little miracles in life than the poor. Therefore, if a person chooses to live in poverty they have no choice but to look to the simple things in life for happiness. Without the distraction of material possessions, the mind is fully focused on how life can provide.

Of course, there are many poor people walking the streets who do not see life this way. They invariably find no solution to their problems in this cold world. However, this is because the poor are reliant on the grace of those who are more fortunate. With more people in the world looking to help the poor and lost, these people would find that life does indeed provide. Again, this relies on people refraining from the natural human tendency to be greedy. Those who have more than enough should feel that they have a duty to share this good fortune with those who are less fortunate. This is another reason to abstain from excess. Those who have more than they need and who hoard it are taking it away from others. This harkens back to the twenty-four inch gauge and its teaching of helping a friend or brother in time of need.

Reducing excess is important, then, because it allows others to partake in what life has to offer when it is not hoarded by the few, and allows us to appreciate that happiness can come from a more sustainable source within.

An active use of the faculty of conscience requires what is known as mindfulness. To be mindful, a person needs to live every moment in full awareness. This continuous attention to every moment involves being aware of every passing thought, everything that leaves our lips, and everything we do.

Much of the time, we live life as though we were on autopilot, and spend very little time actually aware of what we are doing in the present moment. When we are driving, or walking, or working, or anything, our mind tends to be busy attending to something else. For many of us, the mind is out of control.

To remedy this, we have to become aware of each time our mind wanders off to something other than the present moment and what we are doing in that moment, and then pull it back into focus. As we do this over time, we will train our brains to be naturally focused on the here and now. When this is achieved, there are some obvious healthy effects: we tend to worry less, because our mind does not drift to thoughts of anxiety, thus causing our stress levels to be lower; we perform our day-to-day tasks more efficiently because we are not distracted from them; we think more clearly because the thoughts that arise are more relevant to the moment; and we command when our brain thinks, as and when we need to.

Aside from these very positive effects, the clear-thinking aspects of mindfulness allow us to be able to take a step back and watch our thoughts happen. If they are negative or not very useful thoughts, we can discard them in favour of more positive and useful ones. As a result, if we can consciously filter our thoughts we can control our speech, and ensure that what we say is only positive and constructive. Furthermore, our thoughts not only precede our speech, but also our actions. When we have an urge to do something, we can become practised at stepping back and judging the consequences of that action before we commit to it. That way, every action that we allow ourselves to take part in is positive and constructive.

Finally, the concept of living mindfully will help us become aware of our natural faults and help us to use the teachings of the common gavel to reduce their impact upon us. Only by making sure that we live every moment with a sense of being entirely present can we enable our minds to become clear enough to see to the source of our failures. By being vigilant at all times we can see when our faults present themselves, so that we may ward off their impact and replace them with more useful strengths.

'The Chisel'

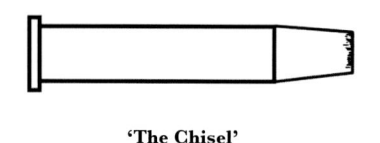

The third working-tool of the First Degree is the chisel. This is a fine-edged tool that is generally used to further smooth a stone after it has been worked on by the rougher common gavel. The chisel allows the stonemason finer control over the look of the finished product before the stone is passed on to be further dressed and included in the building for which it is intended. The purpose of the chisel in Freemasonry is to denote education.

Education enables us to be of use to society in general. The gaining of any kind of knowledge can be useful to us, but the best kind of knowledge is that which we can put into practice and put to good use for those around us. It is important, therefore for a person to strive to continually improve himself in his chosen profession. This requires that a person never consider themselves to be the master of their trade, but to always look for something new that they can learn. The better practised a person can be at their work, the better position they will find themselves in to render services to the community at large.

As we have previously mentioned, Freemasonry refers to the liberal arts and sciences, these being logic, arithmetic, geometry, grammar, rhetoric, music, and astronomy. A Freemason is encouraged to make these areas of study a particular focus, as it is these areas that can properly prepare a mind to understand the world around them. Therefore, although we have touched upon each of these topics in the first chapter, we should discuss them more deeply here.

The first of these arts and sciences is logic, and it is this faculty that allows us to understand the underlying relationship between anything at all. With logic, we are able to discern facts that are not readily accessible to the human senses. One such example is the discovery of 'black holes' in the universe. When Albert Einstein wrote down his theory of general relativity, which explained how gravity worked throughout the universe, he calculated that there should be a type of star so dense that its gravity would be strong enough to stop light from escaping its surface. These types of stars were given the name 'black holes' and the implication of them in the equations of Einstein's theory spurred scientists to look for these entities out in the universe. Since Einstein, we have been able to discern black holes through our powerful telescopes. The point of this is that, through logic, Einstein was able to show that something should exist before we found any direct evidence of it. In the same way, we have taken the evidence that the universe is expanding to imply that it must all have started at some point in the past, in an event called the 'Big Bang.' We have no real direct proof that the Big Bang really happened, but given the mounting evidence and the gift of logic, scientists are feeling quite certain that it all began in this particular way.

Moving from the grandiose to the more everyday, people use logic all of the time to uncover relationships. The police use logic to join together types of evidence to help them solve crimes. A person trying to find their way on a map uses logic to help them find their location on the map from the placement of objects around them. We even use logic when we cross the road by judging the speed of an oncoming car to work out whether it is safe to cross at walking pace, or whether we should move faster.

Logic, then, seems to be something that is innate to our brains. It is something that appears to have evolved to enable us to survive. For instance, if our ancestors heard the roar of a sabre-toothed tiger coming towards them, it would be important to know first, from which direction the roar came, and second to figure out that running in the opposite direction and to safety is probably the best idea. Whilst this might seem obvious and hardly worth mentioning, it is nevertheless important to understand that the simplest things we take for granted require a basic understanding of logic, and that this logic appears not to be taught but seems innate to us.

Some would even go further than this and say that logic is not just innate to the way our brains work, but is written into the very fabric of the universe. Evidence that might be cited for this might include the Golden Ratio or the number 1.618 (rounded to three decimal places). The Golden Ratio is seen everywhere in nature. Take the spiral design of a snail shell: as the spiral design gets bigger each turn of the spiral is 1.618 times further out than the last. This has also been seen to be true of spiral galaxies, of the placement of sunflower seeds in the centre of the petals, and of the placement of the plates on a pineapple. The Golden Ratio is everywhere, as are more familiar numbers such as Pi. For these reasons alone, people have suggested that logic is built into everything around us. If this is the case, then it is important to hone our skill in logic in order to understand the world.

Logic leads nicely into the realm of arithmetic. Arithmetic is essentially what we know as maths and it is the clearest language that human beings have to express the faculty of logic. Arithmetic is built on the very foundation of logic, giving it symbols to speak through.

As we know, the symbol for two things is '2' and when we put these two things together with another two things we see that we have four things in total, represented by the symbol '4'. The symbol '+' has been used to denote the putting of one set of things together with another set, and the symbol ' = ' to denote what the result of this grouping is. This example of course, is neatly written down as 2+2=4, but it can easily be seen how arithmetic expresses logical thought and how it can be made to easily represent general statements about the world. In our example, for instance, it doesn't matter if we have two oranges grouped with two apples, the result is always going to be four things. Once again, this could be a way of showing how logic is inbuilt in the world around us.

Of course, we have symbols for subtraction '-', multiplication 'x', and division '/'. Combined with addition, we have the basics of the language of arithmetic. Using these simple operators we can work out how fast something is moving, how much change we will get after buying something, and when we should put the potatoes on to cook if we need to eat by 2 p.m. Furthermore, the language of arithmetic has been developed much further into areas of mathematics such as calculus, which was developed by Isaac Newton to calculate changes such as acceleration. Through calculus, we can see what the speed of an accelerating object is at any given time on its journey.

Through arithmetic, we can write down the logic of a great many things that enable us to achieve miracles. We can calculate the load-bearing capabilities of materials used in buildings and bridges. We can work out how to put together an engine so that it doesn't explode but instead uses the explosive power of ignited fuel to drive us down the road.

It is important for us to understand arithmetic therefore if we are to manipulate logic in the world. Through even the most basic of arithmetic we can ensure that our endeavours will come to fruition, even before we build anything.

The third of the liberal arts and sciences is geometry. This is a particular application of arithmetic, which deals, in particular, with the relationships between things. A well-known part of geometry is the relationship between the angles of a triangle. We know that all of the angles within a triangle must add up to 180 degrees, and this means that each one of the individual three angles can be anything as long as they add to this number. Another well-known concept of geometry is that expressed in Pythagoras' right-angled triangle: that the square on the hypotenuse is equal to the sum of the squares of the other two sides.

The word 'geometry' means 'earth measurement' and is traditionally concerned with measuring distances between places and objects. Through understanding geometry at this level, we can measure the distances and relationships between objects around us, and scale them down to represent them on maps that we can design on paper.

The first three of the liberal arts and sciences are related to logic and mathematics, and understanding these is key to understanding how the world is built and how we might discern knowledge that is not readily observable. However, this only covers one area of knowledge, which is specifically covered by the right side of the brain. The other side of the brain is dedicated to the more creative aspects of knowledge. Therefore, for a more complete repertoire we must look at the more creative aspects. In the seven liberal arts and sciences, we have two concerned with language and one concerned with music.

The first of the language arts is that of grammar. Grammar is concerned with how language is structured and is crucial to the effective delivery of both oral and written communication. Through the knowledge of grammar, we can place emphasis on particular words or phrases.

Of course, we are all familiar with the tools of grammar such as the full stop, the comma, and the colon. But to be an effective communicator it is important to understand how these tools work so that we can use them to full effect. In this way, we can make our words come alive on the page, or have our spoken words appear pregnant with meaning.

Tied closely with grammar is the art of rhetoric, which is defined as the art of persuasion. The philosopher Aristotle laid down the rules of rhetoric; they were designed to persuade the opponent in any argument. Argument, to Aristotle, was not so much about proving the other person wrong, but rather a way through which both parties could further their knowledge. In order to do this effectively, a person needed to be versed in sufficient techniques for convincing others of their position.

Rhetoric itself is something we are all familiar with, at least at a subconscious level. We are constantly bombarded by well-put-together persuasive arguments in ordinary conversation and speeches, as well as in the media. However, Aristotle put together the formal rules of persuasive communication so that they could be used universally.

Aristotle defined rhetoric as 'the faculty of observing in any given case the available means of persuasion.' Moreover, he saw a convincing argument as being composed with attention to three particular things: the subject, audience, and speaker. In order to put together effective communication, Aristotle thought, a person needed to consider these particular subjects most of all.

Paying attention to the subject of the argument means that the speaker or writer should take into account everything that they know about the particular subject at hand. This means that, before approaching the argument itself, the communicator must take stock of what they already know, and what they need to find out through research.

We have all experienced what it is like to enter a debate, only to be shot down by someone who is more informed than us on the topic. Thorough research, then, is required to ensure that this does not happen and that meaningful progress can be made.

Paying consideration to the audience means that we should ensure we understand the audience that is going to be at the listening or reading end of the communication. If a presentation on some aspect of physics is to be communicated to professional physicists, for instance, one can expect to be free to use technical language, because we take it for granted that this terminology will be understood. Give the same presentation to an audience of non-professional physicists, however, and you might find that people are having a hard time following you, and the presentation will fall flat on its face. In the latter instance, it would be better to dispense with the more technical language in favour of more everyday terms the audience can get their heads round.

Attention to the speaker, or writer, means that the communicator should utilise who they are to express their side of the argument. As people, we all have a unique perspective derived from our own particular experiences in life, and what our personalities are like. No matter how much we have researched, or how much we consider the audience, it is important to put ourselves into a discussion because this is how an audience will connect with us and listen to what we have to say.

Additionally, Aristotle believed that any good argument should pay specific attention to three modes of persuasion, which are called logos, pathos, and ethos.

Logos is the ability to place logic in an argument, so that an audience can follow your reasoning in what you have to say. This generally means that a speaker or writer should break down their point into its constituent parts, and take the audience on a journey to reconstruct them logically, eventually arriving at the central argument.

Pathos is the ability to lend emotion to an argument. Usually, if you can express emotion when giving a speech or communicating in writing then you will invoke similar emotions in the audience. This means that they are more likely to take your particular side in the argument, and it also means they are more likely to remember everything you want to put across.

Finally, Ethos is the ability to communicate an air of authority in your argument. This means establishing that you are well versed in the topic at hand. If an audience sees that you seem to know what you are talking about then they will be more likely to listen to you, and hang on to what you have to say.

In summary, the work of Aristotle in codifying the tenets of effective rhetoric has given us the understanding of how to put together a convincing argument from a psychological perspective. Since the communication of ideas is so important in every aspect of life this is why it is so important to include rhetoric in the all-important liberal arts and sciences.

The next liberal art is music. Music is an interesting psychological phenomenon that seems to be able to shift moods and inspire people in a unique way. It can cause people to weep, or dance with joy. The musical art, then, is the ability to put together sounds in such a way as to move people.

To be an effective musician, a person must understand the grammar of music. This means that they must have an understanding of timings and groupings of notes and sounds in the same way that, in order to be an effective writer, the effective timing and grouping of words must be understood.

Of course, it is not only the grammar of music that should be understood, but also the rhetoric of music. It can be seen that music appeals to an audience's sense of pathos, or emotion, but music also appeals to our sense of logos, or logic, in the way that sounds are placed together and in what sequence. It is possible for almost anyone to identify a harmonious piece of music as being different from one which is discordant, and this is due to the innate logic of music.

In music Ethos, or authority, is communicated by the skill of the musician. Generally speaking, a person can tell the difference between music composed by a near-novice and one produced by an artist with experience.

Therefore, in order to extend our appreciation of the universe around us, music is included in the seven liberal arts and sciences. Indeed, it has even been postulated that the rules of music are written throughout the universe. Since the discovery of the harmonic scale by Pythagoras around 500 BCE, which showed that harmonious notes are found to be placed every eight notes, others have seen this pattern elsewhere. For instance, if the chemical elements from the periodic table are arranged in order of atomic weight, it has been found that every eighth element has similar properties. It is discoveries such as this that show harmony to be everywhere, and therefore make music an art worth studying.

The final liberal art or science is astronomy, which is the science of understanding the composition of the universe and the motion of celestial bodies. Since ancient times it has been believed that the passage of the stars has some relevance to human endeavour, and this is still believed in some quarters today. However, the study of the wider universe allows us to understand the context in which we exist on the tiny blue and green planet of ours.

By observing the wider universe, we have the opportunity to see the universality of the knowledge we have gained in our earthbound existence. It also allows us to ponder the depths of the universe we do not understand, and to marvel at our seeming insignificance in the vastness of time and space.

Although Freemasonry places specific emphasis on the liberal arts and sciences, it is important not to neglect wider subject matters. A Freemason who follows the philosophy diligently will see any newfound knowledge as a useful treasure to acquire.

To summarise the purpose of studying the liberal arts and sciences, we can see that these subjects, in particular, can lead us to a deep understanding of the world around us, and our behaviour within it. By studying these topics, we can prepare ourselves for effective service to others. However, education should not be restricted to these areas of study alone.

Any form of education can render a person a fit member of regularly organised society, therefore the ideal Mason seeks to broaden their knowledge in as many fields as they possibly can, helping to prepare their mind for better use in the world.

Just like the physical body in general, the mind must be trained in order to keep it in peak condition. Technically speaking, the human body is capable of many things, but it must be kept fit in order to express itself fully. We must try to maintain a healthy weight, flexibility, and internal nutritional balance in order that the human body does not impede itself in its function. Every human being is capable of running with a fair amount of ease, and this comes in very useful when running to catch something or running away from danger. When, however, a person carries too much weight, this perfectly natural ability becomes impaired.

In the same way, the human brain is capable of a great many things, with much of its function being subconscious. The brain gets on with ensuring that our respiratory system works effectively, ensures that we can find out way around without bumping into walls, and provides the means to do countless tasks without paying much thought to them. However, the human brain is a tool that can be used for far more applications than the day-to-day existence, and with a properly trained mind, we can utilise it to truly express ourselves in a very wide variety of ways. We cannot for instance, express ourselves musically if we have not trained ourselves in the ways of producing harmonious sounds with particular instruments and we cannot communicate our thoughts effectively if we are not well trained in grammar and rhetoric. We cannot come up with useful ideas about the universe unless we are trained in the known science of astronomy and physics, and we cannot fully explore logic unless we have a full grasp of its underlying ideas and the principles that can be utilised to arrive at conclusions.

Any subject we choose to learn enables us to think and express ourselves more clearly. If we express ourselves more clearly and effectively, we can give more to society, and this is what Freemasonry is all about, namely serving others as effectively as possible.

Educating ourselves also enables us to push ourselves beyond our comfort-zones to explore where our limits truly lie. As we become accomplished in more skills, we learn along the way what we are capable of. Often, we surprise ourselves with what we can do. A person might think that they cannot cook, or learn to play an instrument, or master mathematics, or master any other given skill in which they have no previous experience. However, instead of submitting to a tendency to wallow in what we can't do, one of the implied messages of the chisel is that we should consider ourselves capable of much more if we allow ourselves to be educated in new things. In effect, in pursuing education and stretching our minds, we are finding out more of who we are and, as we have already said, Freemasonry is a tradition that enables a person to look within in a process of self-discovery.

Human beings have come a long way throughout history. From our animalistic and more primitive beginnings we have tamed fire, learned how to make and utilise tools, have built means for shelter anywhere we settle, have built systems of laws, and have organised society into relatively safe places to be as opposed to the raw harshness of nature.

As well as harnessing fire, we have learned to harness other aspects of nature, such as electricity and nuclear energy, allowing us to develop technology that aids us in our day-to-day modern living. We have developed an understanding of the functions of biology that helps us to combat disease that would normally kill us in nature. The entirety of human progress has been built on education in the concepts that others have discovered before us.

We might consider the great philosophers and scientists of the past to be geniuses who have handed down a great deal to us, but they themselves needed to understand what was already known about the world around them before they could build further upon what was known. Albert Einstein couldn't have come up with his theories of relativity without first understanding the principles of relative motion, or the principles of light and electromagnetic radiation. Everything that is invented in society is built upon what has gone before, and so we must understand what is already known in order to progress knowledge, if that is what we want to do.

Even in purely general terms, education is key to society, and this is why Freemasonry defines education as that which renders a person a fit member of organised society. In modern society, it is important for a person to be as educated as possible in at least the basic subjects that our society takes for granted. For instance, in modern times there is a great reliance on the use of computers, mobile devices, and the Internet. A person who is not educated up to at least a basic standard in how to operate these pieces of technology can very quickly find themselves left behind in society.

Children in schools are sometimes better versed in computer technology usage than their parents, which is only natural because, whether one thinks this a good thing or a bad thing, the future looks to become more technologically driven.

As life changes, so people should change in order to adapt and maintain themselves as fit members of society in its modern form, and by ensuring we are educated in mathematics and communication skills at the very least, as well as the more specialist subjects, we can do our part in ensuring the advancement of humanity into the future generations.

In the use of these symbolic tools, it should perhaps be remembered that the mediaeval stonemasons rarely used these tools on their own. The tools of the First Degree are supposed to be used together. One obvious example of this is the chisel, since it is difficult to imagine how one might use a chisel without a hammer or mallet to knock it with. Of course, the first set of tools we have at our disposal includes the common gavel, which is not only designed to knock away unnecessary rough parts of a stone block but may also be used to provide power when refining the stone further with the sharp edge of the chisel. If the chisel represents the advantages of education and the common gavel represents the force of conscience, then perhaps the use of them together could be considered to represent the process of conscientiously applied education.

Conscientiously applying education to ourselves means to understand what we do know and what we don't know. It also implies that we should understand what we need to know in order to be as serviceable as we can be.

As we refine ourselves with education, we are guiding that process with our innate sense of conscience.

Finally, we have the first tool of this set: the twenty-four inch gauge, which represents the twenty-four hours of the day. Using this in combination with the gavel and chisel means that we must measure how much material we have to work with before we begin crafting and honing. The material being worked with here is time.

As the Mason spends their time crafting themselves conscientiously and with a mind to education they are encouraged to ensure that they are dividing their specific focus between matters of spirituality, general work and labour, and service to others. In each of these areas we can educate ourselves to become more proficient, and in each of these areas too we can guide ourselves with the faculty of conscience, which can highlight to us where we have been lacking.

The working-tools of the First Degree, then, are all tools of change. They are all about the crafting of a person into a more ideal form that can be more serviceable to humanity as a whole. The repeated use of the twenty-four inch gauge, common gavel, and chisel will enable the Freemason to shape themselves in a process of daily self-improvement.

However, we must understand that this crafting process should be directed in a particular direction. The Mason is attempting to knock off the rough parts of themselves, in order to complete the progression to the perfect ashlar, which represents a person who is fulfilled and serviceable. The Freemason needs to know, therefore, what shape to craft themselves into, and this requires tools of measurement, and it is these tools that will be the focus of the next chapter.

CHAPTER 4

THE WORKING-TOOLS OF THE SECOND DEGREE

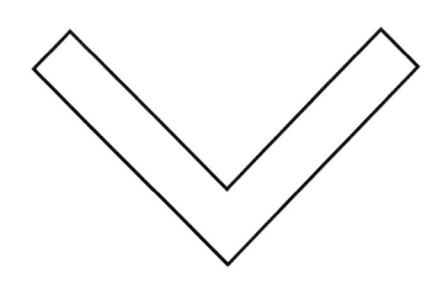

'The Square'

The Second Degree in Freemasonry is called the Fellow Craft Degree. If the First Degree is about initiation into Freemasonry, then the emphasis of the Fellow Craft Degree is about living the Masonic life, but what exactly does this mean?

As we have previously discussed, Freemasonry is all about personal change into a person who is able to give more of themselves in life. In order to do this, Freemasons need to craft themselves using the techniques implied by the first set of working-tools. However, crafting oneself with tools of change is not sufficient on its own: the Mason also constantly needs to ensure that they are moving towards their final goal as they craft. In order to do this, care needs to be taken to make sure that the self-crafting Initiate is constantly measuring their progress to see if they are deviating at all from the path they wish to follow.

Operative stonemasons, who would work on stone with chisels and gavels, needed to ensure they were continuously measuring how the stone was changing shape so they could determine how close they were getting to the finished product. The ultimate goal for the stonemason was to create a smooth ashlar, i.e. a block of stone that is perfectly cuboid in shape. This meant that the edges of the smooth ashlar had to be perfect ninety-degree angles, and the sides to be perfectly smooth, so that it could fit together exactly with the other ashlars that would go into making the building.

In order to ensure that their work was progressing in the right direction the stonemasons would employ three main tools of measurement, namely the square, level, and plumb rule, and it is these, which comprise the working-tools of the Second Degree in Freemasonry.

In this chapter, then, we will see how each of these tools of the operative fellow craft stonemason can be interpreted symbolically in order for the Freemason to measure their progress on their journey of personal transformation.

The first of the Second Degree working-tools is the square. This tool is utilised to ensure that corners and edges of an ashlar block being worked upon are right-angles, i.e. angles of ninety degrees. The square, then, is a tool that is continuously set at ninety degrees so that it can be pressed up against a workpiece to see if it fits the template.

In speculative Freemasonry, the square denotes morality and, in many ways, this concept has fed into everyday usage. For instance, the morally correct thing to do in any given situation is often called the 'right' thing to do, a term that can be seen to come from Masonic origins when we understand how the ninety-degree right-angle can be seen to represent morality. There are many other common phrases that show how the square represents morality, such as getting a square deal, squaring off, everything being all square, and so on.

In Freemasonry, the Mason is encouraged to act with other people 'on the square', which means to act with them firmly in balance and in fairness. In essence, this is to act with the Golden Rule of doing to others as we would have them do to us, which is a very straightforward way of ensuring that our behaviour is honourable towards others. If we would not like something done to us, no matter what it might be, we perhaps shouldn't do that same thing to other people.

This rule has existed throughout the history of mankind, and all over the world. In the fifth century BCE, the Great Learning, one of the revered old books of China, instructed that a man should not do unto others what he would not have them do unto him. Many of us understand the Golden Rule to be Christian in origin, through the teachings of Jesus, but it is clear that such ideas were around long before the Christian era and in different parts of the world.

It would appear, then, that the principle of the square is universal amongst human beings, and it doesn't seem to be restricted to our species. Anyone who has ever owned a dog knows that they understand when they have done something that their owners might consider bad, even if they haven't been told off for it before.

No one really understands where our moral intuition comes from, but perhaps it is the ability to imagine how we would feel in given moral situations. Doing good can be defined as reducing suffering or causing joy, and doing bad can be seen as doing the exact opposite. It is in this way that all human beings have an understanding of what good and evil is, and so, irrespective of whether we have experienced the moral dilemma before, we appear able to follow through the consequences of our actions in our minds to determine whether it will cause harm or reduce suffering of some description.

The ability to conceptualise the consequences of our actions clearly has something to do with our moral behaviour, since it can be shown that it is possible to do great harm when we act without being properly informed. A small child, for instance, who is fairly new to this world, might think nothing of taking a toy off another child and start playing with it, or taking another child's sweets and eating them. In these and similar instances we tend to give our children a certain amount of room in our judgements, as we understand that they are innocent and that they haven't learned that these things are wrong. Parents showing their approval and disapproval as situations arise teach the right and wrong of such actions.

Ignorance can also be seen as a precursor to immorality in human history. In modern times, we are very concerned about our effect on our planet's environment. Nowadays, we have to separate our rubbish into recyclable and non-recyclable, we have to ensure that new buildings leave a low carbon footprint in their daily function, and we no longer use ozone-damaging chemicals. All of this is intended to reduce the amount of damage to the natural world in which we live. The preservation of the environment is largely considered a good thing.

In contrast to the greener behaviour found in modern living, human history shows us that we have not always been as kind to the world we call home. During the Industrial Revolution, when factories were built that would billow smoke and steam into the skies, we gave little to no thought as to what the long-term effects of these things would be. The only thing that human beings were concerned with was human progress.

We all know that damaging the environment can be considered a very bad thing but, in context, human beings hadn't stopped to consider the damage to the environment or its consequences. It wasn't until research started to suggest that damage was occurring that anyone thought to give a care to the environment, and this only because we started to realise how this damage would affect our comfort and survival in the long term. Once again, it was ignorance that allowed us to cause harm through negligence, a situation that is slowly being repaired through being more informed.

Another thing that we consider morally bad in our modern era is the mistreating of animals. Nowadays we are very concerned with how we treat members of other species we share our planet with but, in the past, this was not so much the case. Historically, human beings have been convinced that they are the dominant species on the planet and that the environment, including the other animals within it, should be subjugated to us. This error of thought perhaps came from the idea that we were different to animals.

Again, as science has progressed, especially with the work of people like Charles Darwin, we have come to understand the natural world even more and have come to respect the fact that we are as much animals as the rest of the animal kingdom. This has enabled us to sympathise with the plight of other species, especially those that come into direct contact with human beings.

Our understanding of our relationship to animals and the interconnection we have with the natural world has even driven us to care for animals that appear to be becoming extinct. Humankind appears to wish to undo what it has done in the past. This can only be seen as a morally good thing, but it is one that has come from the dispelling of ignorance.

As our understanding grows both on a wider and on a more personal level, we seem to be better able to understand that everything in the world is connected in some way. An individual's actions in the world have a profound effect on the world around them, and the ability to understand just what these effects are means that we can judge whether they can be considered constructive or detrimental, and regulate our actions accordingly.

Simply put, we are talking about living life in a more mindful state. By taking the time to think through the consequences of their actions and judging these outcomes by placing themselves in the shoes of those on the receiving end, a person can keep themselves on a morally correct path, which can only have a positive impact on the individuals that they come into contact with.

Compassion also comes into the lesson of the square. The term 'square' essentially means to be equal-sided. As we learn that everyone around us is essentially the same as us, we can understand that these humans feel roughly the same as us in similar situations. The Freemason, then, through understanding their equality with others, is invited to reach out in assistance to his fellow human and to alleviate any potential suffering they might see occurring, informed by their assessment on how such a situation would make them feel.

Since we have mentioned equality, now is a good time to move on to the next working-tool in the Fellow Craft Degree, which is called the level.

In operative masonry, the level is a tool that enables the stonemason to 'prove horizontals.' In other words, the stone-worker uses the level to make sure that the stone surface they are working on is perfectly horizontal, or level. Clearly, this is a very important concern when constructing the elements of a building. If each of the stone blocks that are to comprise the building are not level then the building itself will not be level, and the whole structure would be in danger of collapsing.

In speculative Freemasonry, the property of being level is seen to represent equality. Every human being is considered equal, which means that we are all

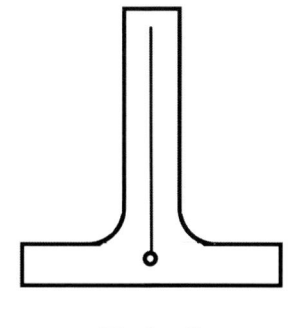

'The Level'

partakers of the same essential facts of life. All of us are born into a world filled with joy, sorrow, pleasure, pain, abundance, lack, health, sickness, abundant life, and death. Regardless of who we are, or what we can do, we all get sick, feel pain, feel loss and sorrow and, eventually, must face death.

However, the fact that we are all subject to the ups and downs of life is quite often forgotten because we are all presented with the evidence that lies all around us that people are not equal. There are very wealthy people in the world who seem to be able to enjoy every good thing that the world can offer. Some people are born into this world with privilege and financial security, whilst others receive it through luck and others through the results of their own endeavour.

By contrast, there are people who are without homes and are forced to live in the cold, and people who don't know where their family's next meal is coming from. Clearly, from a financial perspective, people are by no means equal.

When we look at the world around us, we tend to take the concepts it presents for granted. For instance, all human beings have a concept of ownership, but what, exactly, does ownership actually mean? When a person buys something, in what real measure is it 'theirs'? Take a shiny new car, for example, which has been acquired from a showroom. Certainly, this vehicle may very well cater to the needs of the owner to travel around. However, we all accept that this same vehicle will eventually begin to require more and more service and repair and, eventually, will break down and disappear altogether into a pile of rusted metal. What is being 'owned' here? A car that has had its timing-belt changed is not the car that was first purchased, because the original belt has been replaced, and so on, as more and more bits and pieces are replaced.

Ownership, therefore, does not pertain to actual objects it seems, but instead to concepts of objects. The very meaning of ownership seems to be a vague set of rules invented by mankind itself. This extends to other forms of ownership, like the owning of land. The only reason one person owns several acres of land and another person none at all is because the landowner has placed a fence around a chunk of land on the planet and, by agreement, can call it theirs. It is not really theirs, however, because one day they will pass away and this land will stand, still with its imagined border, without the original owner in existence.

It would seem, then, a rich person is only rich because society has set up a system by which people can enter into agreements of ownership. In reality, the materially rich stand equally with the materially poor when looked at from a non-human world perspective.

There are so many forms of inequality around us, whether they are aesthetic, physical, social, or intellectual, so how does Freemasonry teach its Initiates a contrary lesson to what the world appears to be showing them?

In essence, the lesson of the level is one of perspective and an adjustment of a person's perspective. Each of us, no matter who we are, are on our own personal journeys through life. None of these journeys is identical, but the simple fact that we have all been cast into life without any clue as to what it is all about, and will all face our own challenges and triumphs, is exactly what every human being has had in common with all others throughout all of human history.

Imagine an athlete who has worked very hard to be good enough to be accepted to run in the Olympic Games. This athlete has had to commit a lot of time to their cause, which means that they have sacrificed much of everything else in order to realise their dreams.

They may not have been able to spend as much time as they would prefer around their friends and family, or perhaps they have had to fight the temptation to not practice because they have had a bad day, or have other priorities which demand their attention. Whatever the details of this specific journey, there are clearly many challenges on the road to athletic success. The medal they might achieve at the end makes it all worthwhile.

Now consider another athlete with the same goal of competing in the Olympics. Unfortunately, this athlete suffers a tragic road accident, which results in him losing both of his legs. This person immediately has our sympathies. Suddenly, on top of the challenges of the previous athlete, he has lost the very tools of his trade, causing very severe physical and psychological obstacles. This person could choose to go two ways: give up and do something else whilst coping with what life has dealt them, or they could choose to look their tragedy in the eye and swear not to be beaten. Fortunately, our injured athlete decides to do the latter. He gets fitted with prosthetic attachments that he can use as replacement legs, continues to train, making allowances for his new equipment and circumstances, and enters the Para Olympics.

These are very different approaches to the same goal, with different obstacles and challenges. The point is that neither of their spirits was broken by those challenges, even in the case of the unfortunate second athlete. Both of their ambitions were realised, even though one had further to go. Even though the two athletes' circumstances were very unequal, their inner cores were fairly equal: they were both determined to make themselves into Olympic athletes. Thankfully, for the disabled athlete, technology and mind-sets were available for him to continue his career.

This is one of the lessons of the level. It teaches us that human beings should be considered equal in spirit, even if their journeys and associated challenges are quite different. Regardless of circumstances, every human being should have the opportunity to make of themselves whatever they wish. It is the job of humanity in general to remove the obstacles that might otherwise prevent the realisation of dreams. Therefore, the Freemason should be a person who understands the equality of each human being and, if they are able, should try to offer assistance in the removal of their identified obstacles. It is only with this attitude that humanity can push its own boundaries and strive to be something more and, indeed, the best that humanity can be.

As well as the many challenges that face us in our lives, the arena where we most experience pressing inequalities is that of a social nature. We all understand and have possibly even met snobbish people i.e. those people who appear to think that they are in some way superior to others.

These people might be intelligent and knowledgeable and might be the type of person who looks down on those who are not so gifted. Unfortunately, these people are under an illusion: when you think about it, there is very little difference between the most knowledgeable person in the world and the least. If we consider any of the areas of knowledge, it is very clear that progress is being made. For instance, science has brought us the many privileges of technology. However, even the most gifted physicists are still looking for the secrets of how the universe came into being, and this means that there is a limit to our understanding of anything we can study in the universe. Eventually, we come to a point where no science can provide answers. On top of this, as has been mentioned in a previous chapter, the understanding that science can provide can only take us back to the moment that the universe sprang into being. Even if all of the equations that explain how everything proceeded from the moment the universe started are discovered and understood, we still need to ask why these equations exist. Then if we answer this, we need to answer why this is the case, and so on in an ongoing process called the infinite regress. It would seem that it is impossible to imagine that the human mind will ever truly grasp the answers to everything in the traditional rational manner. It may even be the case that there is no cause; something that is an affront in itself to the human ego. Perhaps everything needs a cause from the human perspective, because we are used to dealing with a causal world, but what if the same logic doesn't apply to the universe?

The point of all this is that if the underlying workings of the universe ultimately transcend human understanding, then nothing definitive can really be said about anything. All of the knowledge we take for granted, then, is mere approximations to the truth, useful though these approximations are. In this sense, at some point, the most knowledgeable people in the world are struck as dumb as those who are considered 'dumb'. This realisation is a great leveller within intellectual circles. Intellectual snobs, be advised!

The other classic form of snobbery is that of the materially rich over the materially poor. However, it is perhaps important to remember that, no matter how much wealth a person has, it can easily be taken away when the wider economic environment changes. People without great wealth could even be considered to be more in touch with their own humanity as they are not distracted by the facade that material wealth can bring. It is all too easy to be convinced by the illusory assumed status that wealth can bring. It is easier for the wealthy to see themselves as different from those around them. The poorer in society are not burdened by such an illusion. It is perhaps no coincidence that there tends to be a greater sense of community amongst the less wealthy than amongst the better off.

More generally, throughout history, there have been many tragic appearances of inequality. None have been more pervasive than racial and religious inequality. Human beings seem to have a history of being unable to register the basic humanity we all share. Those who are racially different have historically been treated as inferior, and therefore only fit for subordination as servants and slaves. Racism has even been the cause of genocide in many different parts of history.

All of this, of course, was caused through ignorance. Since someone looked different, it was believed that they were different. Thankfully this ignorance has been swept away and we have recognised that the differences are only skin-deep and that, inside, all human beings are essentially the same and deserve to be treated with respect.

As racial discrimination is being gradually eroded, religious inequality seems to still be very prominent. Those who are of particular denominations or faiths seem to believe that they are members of the one true faith. Of course, there can be no guarantee that any of the faiths of the world are uniquely in possession of the truth. There are so many faiths of the world and it would appear that, at their core, they speak of the same basic truths. Their differences appear to emerge from the fact that the various religions have emerged from different cultures in different geographical regions of the world.

The aim of each of the faiths appears to be to teach basic human morality and to move closer to the transcendent reality that lies behind all things that has been called, or is at least represented by, the deity. Therefore, it should be possible for the faiths to respect each other's unique qualities and yet still understand that they are saying the same thing. However, the world seems rife with religiously motivated strife. Wars are fought in the name of religious differences and there is civil unrest where one group of religious believers have directly attacked, sometimes physically, those of a different faith.

The problem with religious inequality appears to stem from those who feel that their particular religious scripture should be interpreted literally, as the literal truth. With so many different faiths, and within each a group of people insisting on literal interpretation to the exclusion of anything else, it can easily be seen why human beings can look upon their own faith in such territorial ways. Although it is not always popular, the idea of understanding faith in terms of symbolism with only metaphorical import does tend to help with the idea of including disparate faiths. Each item of scripture then becomes empowered and filled with important messages built into the subtext of the story that is too often taken literally.

Evidence for the idea that scriptures were meant to be taken metaphorically can be seen everywhere. In the Old Testament, for instance, there appears to be an overarching theme of leaving a place, going on a journey, then returning. One such example is the sacking of King Solomon's Temple by the Babylonian king Nebuchadnezzar. Once the Babylonians had overtaken Jerusalem, the uprooted Jewish people spent many years in exile in Babylon. Eventually, though, they returned to the 'promised land' to build a new temple. Taken metaphorically, we can see that Jerusalem can be seen as the spiritual home of the Jews. The city included a temple, which was believed, literally, to be the house of God. Being forced out of this spiritual home can be seen to reflect humankind's expulsion from the spiritual paradise he once enjoyed, as represented by the Garden of Eden. The years in exile, then, can be seen to represent man's existence in a state separated from his spiritual source, trying to eke out a life without it, and attempting to work out a way back. Eventually, the way back becomes apparent and a return is effected back to Jerusalem. This, then, is representative of man's eventual return to his spiritual source.

When reading the text in this way, the metaphors can be seen to apply to mankind as a whole or as an individual. The journey of a symbolically chosen people can be seen to represent our separation from spirit prior to our birth, the exile as our lives, and the return as our eventual absorption into the spiritual source after our deaths.

In the realm of non-religious books, it is generally observed that the same stories are repeated over and over again, in many forms of expression. The same underlying truths can be explored by any number of novels in their own way, and using their own metaphors, without people having to resort to insisting that one particular literary expression is the only one that has explored that truth properly. In fact, knowledge of each of the individual novels that explore the same themes can help deepen our understanding of these truths that we all wrestle to understand.

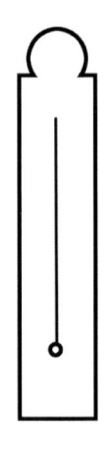

Perhaps, then, religions should be seen in this way, too. Each one of the faiths having their own narrative and story that attempts to tackle the mystery of existence in its own way. It is then that all faiths can come together in common, despite their obvious difference. Each religion and people can exist on a level with each other.

The final working-tool associated with the Second Degree, or Fellow Craft, is the plumb rule. As a tool for the mediaeval stonemason, this was used to ensure that when stone blocks were placed onto their bases in the construction of a building they could be proved to be

'The Plumb Rule'

perfectly upright or perpendicular. If this were not the case then the edifice being built would more than likely lean, succumb to the effects of gravity and fall down.

From the moral perspective, the plumb rule is meant to represent the morally upright person. This means that the Freemason who properly contemplates the meaning of the symbolic plumb rule continually strives to be honest, trustworthy, and principled in their day-to-day conduct. In many ways, the symbolism of the upright stone structure is apt. As human beings, we are a mixture of the lofty ideals of civilisation and the more primitive forces of our more animalistic sides, especially since morality appears to be a human construct that tends to wrestle with our baser natures. Gravity, in this context, represents our ever-present natures that tempt us to move away from the carefully constructed path of morality.

It is so very clear that when systems of government collapse the uglier side of humanity reveals itself. During such periods of lawlessness, human beings seem to enter into such crimes as theft, breaking and entering, and crimes that are far worse and unspeakable. It seems as if there lies beneath the surface of each of us an innate quality that concerns itself only with selfish and immediate concerns.

This aspect of humanity would seem to make sense in the context of evolution. The natural world is a very harsh place to be, and most wild animals appear to be in a constant state of hunger and fear. Food can be very hard to come by, since there is a constant need to pursue sources of nourishment and to protect oneself from the constant threat of predators.

Before civilisation dawned for human beings we were in this wild state, and these same things were probably the dominant subjects in our mind. Naturally, certain aspects of morality arose in order to ensure individuals could be included in the safety of the group. However, the need to think selfishly was obvious because our lives were constantly under threat. Therefore, our nervous systems have evolved in order to protect us, and therefore we have a predisposition to act selfishly.

The psychologist Carl Jung called this aspect of our personality 'The Shadow.' According to Jung, this Shadow contains all of the parts of ourselves that we dare not admit to, and represents our more animalistic natures. However, Jung suggested that it isn't just our own survival that we are interested in. In this system, whenever we think about doing something good, we cannot help but have the opposite action lurking somewhere at the back of the mind. For instance, if you were to see an injured bird on the path in front of you and you picked it up, you might think that you needed to seek help to nurse this animal back to health. However, somewhere in your mind, Jung suggests, is the idea of you closing your hand and ending the bird's life. Any morally decent person reading this will be instantly moved to try to deny that this is true, but that is exactly why Jung called this part of the human mind the Shadow, because it contains all of those things that we would prefer to be kept unseen, even by ourselves.

Jung goes on to suggest further that, if a person denies that this dark side is an inherent part of them, the chances are that the individual will develop a complex later on. Therefore, it is healthy to admit that we are all capable of darker actions, even if we only acknowledge the possibility.

Like the force of gravity, this ever-present shadow aspect of the human personality is always tugging at our resolve to be upright, and life seems filled with times when our morality is tested. Remaining upright, then, can be a tremendous challenge due to the continuous pull of our ever-present, inner natures, which have a tendency to move us back to our naturally selfish states.

It would seem that there is not one system of morality but many, and many of these are restricted to certain groups of humanity. Therefore, if the Freemason is to attempt to remain upright and true to their moral convictions, surely it is important to ensure that these convictions are as far-reaching as possible across the entire gamut of humanity. Indeed, if Freemasonry does not draw distinctions between people of different religious and political backgrounds, then each Freemason should follow a path of morality that benefits all, without variation. How, then, can we arrive at such an all-inclusive morality?

A good starting point for this is the so-called Golden Rule, which states that one should do unto others as we would wish them to do to us. The reason this is a good starting point is that, as individuals, we each have a good idea of what kind of treatment from others allows us to be happy.

Clearly, no normally functioning person would willingly allow pain to be inflicted on themselves by others and therefore - given that human beings generally have the same wishes regarding well-being – we should not inflict pain on others if we can help it. Of course, such a rule is called into question when we have to provide first aid or medical aid to another, which might include the inflicting of temporary pain, but this is moderated by the judgement-call that, without treatment, the situation could become worse for the patient.

In terms of morality, the human species should focus on what is the best thing for each individual on the planet. Some very simple needs must be met if we are to have a chance at being happy as human beings. These needs were identified by Abraham Maslow in his Hierarchy of Needs.

The Hierarchy of Needs covers five stages. The first of these stages covers physiological needs, namely air, food, drink, shelter, warmth, sex, and sleep. These are all very important requirements that a human being should have in order to pursue any kind of normal life.

If we are to ensure that these basic needs are met, human beings should ensure that everything within their power is done in order to provide them. This, then, is a guide to moral behaviour that serves the physiological well-being of humanity in general.

Once the physiological needs have been met, there are then the needs of individual safety. These comprise protection from the elements achieved by providing shelter, security, order, law, stability, and freedom from fear.

When we look at the world around us, it might seem that we fall at the second hurdle. Throughout the world, there are still people without adequate protection from the weather, there are those living in countries without law, order, or stability, and certainly, there are those who live their daily lives in fear.

In order to get over the second obstacle, it is imperative that each individual should work towards ensuring that these things are in place within the scope of their own lives. Of course, which particular laws should be upheld are always areas for contention; however, laws should be there to serve human good and so should directly feed into upholding the human hierarchy of needs.

Next up the hierarchy are needs of belonging and love, comprising of friendship, intimacy, affection, and love. Specifically these needs should be seen as coming from the group with which people work, families, friends and romantic relationships. This level of need is clearly talking about the need for human relationships. It would seem that human beings are social creatures and we can see why this is. The human infant comes into this world completely helpless and entirely reliant on those around it to ensure that its needs are met. In order to ensure that new-born babies get the care they need, human groups have to be close and collaborative. Mothers need support, and the whole support group requires their own needs to be attended to.

If we accept that the most important thing for the human organism is to survive and reproduce, it becomes obvious that human beings have evolved social cravings for just this purpose. Therefore, to remain happy, the human being should be able to live in an environment where these natural instincts to gather with other people in close bonds can be nurtured and fulfilled. Overall, looking after this particular set of needs will have a more global and positive effect on the rest of the human race.

According to Maslow, the fourth level in the hierarchy is concerned with the needs of self-esteem. In order to fulfil this level a human being should be able to strive for achievement, mastery, independence, status and self-respect. It is important to understand here that status does not necessarily mean to lord it over other human beings; it merely means that a human being should be able to strive for the ability to contribute to society in a unique way.

The last level in the original Hierarchy of Needs relates to self-actualisation. This means that a person should be able to attempt to realise personal potential, self-fulfilment, and to seek personal growth and peak experiences. Essentially, this means that a human being should be able to find themselves in a position to explore what their own unique contributions to society can be.

One of the aims of self-actualisation is to seek peak experiences. A peak experience is an event in a person's life that causes their consciousness suddenly to feel a profound sense of the interconnectedness of all things. Usually, an individual experiencing the peak experience feels a profound mixture of feelings. Sometimes, these feelings might include laughter and tears simultaneously. Whatever the experience at the time, it always accompanies a profound sense of peace and understanding. Unfortunately, the peak experience only lasts a few moments and, once it has passed, the person who has experienced it cannot find a way back to the feeling. In fact, there seems to be no way to remember or access the thoughts and feelings that seemed so profound. All that is left in the afterglow is the sense that a person has had a profound experience. Therefore, there is an urge to want to return to the peak experience.

Abraham Maslow felt that a person could find ways to increase the number of peak experiences in their lives, and that it is theoretically possible to maintain a plateau experience, where the sense of profound fulfilment lasts without ebbing away. Achieving the plateau experience, however, would perhaps take a lifetime of training in cultivating the mysterious peak experience. A way of cultivating the number of peak experiences in life is to find those areas of life that enable a person to feel a deep interconnectedness with the world around them. To this end spiritual practice, combined with active involvement in the community, has often been found to be a source of deep insight into the inner meaning of an individual's life.

It is clear, then, that these five levels of need can be seen to be a guide to how human beings become happy. The goal of an overall morality should therefore be one that inclusively protects all of these needs and drives human progress forward in an attempt at better gratifying them. It shouldn't matter where we get our morality from. Whatever the source, a set of morals should be measured against how it serves human well-being, for every individual and for all of humankind.

Morality should not be about how to follow some set of rules given to us by someone or something else. A moral code should flow from a deep understanding of the nature of human beings themselves, as has been done in studies like those undertaken by Maslow. In this regard, there is a clear opportunity afforded to the Freemason.

If Freemasonry is a system of contemplation and mindfulness, which is illustrated and illuminated by symbols, then the practised Freemason should be able to discern his true nature. He should be able to understand what it is that makes him human and thus what will make him happy and, in understanding these things, he should then be able to see that these essential principles lie at the heart of every other human being. With this information, the Freemason can then better appreciate where their efforts are required in order to communicate happiness as far and wide as possible.

This, then, is the lesson of upright intentions that is illustrated by the plumb rule. As we look within to become mindful of our inherent human natures that may tempt us to act selfishly, we can also become mindful of the fact that we have the same basic requirements of happiness as everyone else around us, and that we can help our own happiness by improving the happiness of others through our actions. When we see that people are happy as a result of our efforts, a reward of satisfaction comes which is difficult to gain from any other source. Only through the helping of others and a genuine wish to improve the lives of those around us, otherwise known as upright intentions, can we feel our true value in life, and from the satisfaction of realised purpose comes deep happiness.

An important question arises here. Can one person genuinely make a difference with their upright intentions? The answer to this has to be yes. Simply by existing in society we can have a profound effect. To try to explain this, imagine a time where you have helped someone in your life. It could be anything, offering to lend someone money to get home, giving someone a lift home when they needed it, or giving someone advice on what they need to do. Imagine that you never existed at all. Any time that you have stepped in to help someone simply wouldn't happen. The people's lives would have been made slightly worse by your absence. Furthermore, the people that have been helped by you could perhaps have been inspired to help others. If enough people do this, we can end up with a society where everyone is inspired to lend a hand to others in the name of them finding happiness. We end up with a happier society. It is therefore easy to see that acting with upright intentions and in the interests of those around us is the only way that we can improve society.

As with the working-tools of the First Degree of Freemasonry, the tools of the Second Degree are meant to be used in conjunction with each other, as well as with the tools of the previous Degree. As we have seen, the tools of the Second Degree are all about measuring progress. The ashlar that represents the individual is slowly being crafted into shape by the active tools of the First Degree, but progress towards the end-goal of the smooth ashlar can't be known unless tools of measurement are used.

In every event in our lives that involves other people, the first tool of measurement to use is the plumb rule. With upright intentions we can try to be our very best as we interact with others. Perhaps the best way of approaching anyone is with a genuine wish that they be happy, or to render them the best service possible. To help in this endeavour, the lesson of the square comes along; this ensures that we are doing to others as we would wish others to do to us. The upright intentions that the Mason has are thus supported by a framework with which to construct moral behaviour, based on an understanding of what makes them happy as a human being, which is essentially to act as they would wish people to act in an ideal world. Further supporting the square and the plumb rule as they work together is the level and its lesson of equality.

Equality ensures the moral lesson of the square is used when dealing with everyone, without exception. Similarly, it ensures that no human being lies outside the morally upright aims of the individual Freemason. Regardless of who a person is, where they come from, their background, gender, socio-economic status, or intelligence, everyone deserves to be treated with upright intentions and with due morals.

Of course, none of us is perfect. As we move through life, no matter how upright our intentions are, we are bound to have slips and disappoint ourselves. However, it is at this point that the Freemason, who is attempting to craft themselves into a better person morally, should be mindful enough to understand that they have fallen off the intended path, and that further work needs to be done. This further work is aided by the tools of crafting, as outlined in the Entered Apprentice, or First Degree. If we have done something to someone else that we know we would not like to have had done to us, or if we have acted in some way that hasn't been in the interest of the other party, or if we have held back from assisting someone in need because of mere prejudice, then we should listen to the voice of our conscience, represented by the common gavel, and educate ourselves to act more kindly, represented by the chisel, ever remembering that we should be mindful of the lesson of the twenty-four inch gauge and act to serve those around us in time of need.

In the context of moral self-improvement, the first two Degrees in Freemasonry are very much about working directly on the rough ashlar that represents the Self. In principle, the six working-tools of the Entered Apprentice Degree and the Fellow Craft Degree should be all we need to move towards the perfect ashlar, representing the more morally refined Self. However, this is all very well and good if we are only interested in self-development and nothing else. However, as has already been implied, each individual is inextricably intertwined with other people in society. Everything we do affects those around us. Therefore, it is important that we consider how we are going to make use of ourselves once we have refined ourselves. We need to be able to refine, not only ourselves, but also how we see ourselves in relation to the rest of society.

CHAPTER 5

THE WORKING-TOOLS OF THE THIRD DEGREE

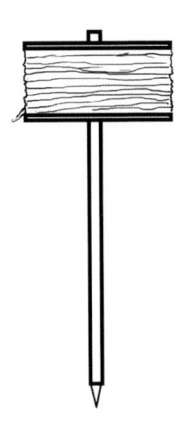

'The Skirret'

As the journey of Freemasonry progresses, it becomes clear that the Degrees seem to be representing the human individual and their journey through life. The First Degree represents an individual's entry into the society of Freemasonry. It is an initiation because it marks the beginning of a new phase in the new Freemason's life, a point where the old rules of life are augmented by a new set of guidelines. Putting it another way, initiation is meant to represent a kind of rebirth into a morally mindful life. The First Degree, then, can be seen to represent the birth of an individual into the world.

Following the First Degree comes the Second, which appears to represent the journey of the Masonic life. One of the more beautiful symbols in Freemasonry appears in this Degree and takes the form of a winding staircase. The particular winding staircase in Freemasonry is one that leads from the ground floor of King Solomon's Temple to the middle chamber of that temple. We will be discussing this building in more detail in a later chapter. The Freemason symbolically ascends this staircase to arrive at the middle chamber. In other words, as a Freemason improves themselves morally, represented by the ascending journey, they are also slowly uncovering their true inner selves, represented by the destination of the middle chamber. Eventually, after a considerable time of self-study, the Freemason will arrive at a realisation of themselves at their very core. The life of the Mason is one of mindful self-discovery and moral improvement. Following the birth of the Entered Apprentice in the First Degree, then, comes the representation of the path of life.

Before moving to the final Degree, we should deal with why this staircase is a winding one. When a person ascends a winding staircase, they cannot easily see around the corner. In addition, they cannot easily see round the corner behind them. The only thing visible to them is the step they are standing on and perhaps the steps immediately in front and behind. This is intended to represent the fact that, as we move through life, we cannot know what the future holds, and we cannot directly perceive our past but must rely on our memories. The only relevant moment is now. As we move, we inhabit one moment at a time, never knowing truly what the next one will hold. Therefore, the Freemason is reminded to be completely mindful of the present and to keep moving forward.

The Third Degree in Freemasonry has a more sombre tone and explores the inevitable destiny of each human being. However, this is merely used as a context for living life morally. If human life is limited, then it is important to use the time we have to impact upon the world as much as we can in a positive way.

Following the six tools of the previous two Degrees, three of direct self-crafting and three of guidance and measurement, the three working-tools of the Third Degree have a wider perspective. The tools are the skirret, the pencil, and the compasses. Where the previous stonemasons' tools are used to work on the individual components of the intended structure, the working-tools of the Third Degree are directed towards the building of the structure as a whole, within the context of the ground on which it is to be built. Symbolically, these tools put everything that has gone before into context.

The first of these tools, the skirret, is a pin or post that has a rotating mechanism on top of it that allows a line to be unwound. In the use of actual stonework and the building of structures, this tool is used to help mark out the ground according to the architectural plan, so that the building blocks can be placed correctly and to ensure the alignment of the building as a whole.

Clearly, this tool creates a relationship between the drawn plan on which the building was first designed and the actual ground on which the real building is to be built. To interpret this tool symbolically, then, we must understand the symbolism of the building and the architectural plans.

Firstly, we should understand that the building represents society as a whole, with each building block representing an individual within society. Once this is understood, it naturally follows that the architectural plans represent a scheme to help that society to come together in an orderly structure. Therefore, the skirret is the tool that communicates that scheme to the actual individuals within society so that they understand their place within that scheme.

Where, then does this scheme come from? Freemasonry suggests that it can be found in the Volume of the Sacred Law. The Volume of the Sacred Law itself, in Freemasonry, is a symbol to represent the central scripture in a Freemason's particular faith. It is understood that the harmonious structure of society has its prototype laid down in the spiritual books of the world. The implication is that if the Freemason studies his particular volume of the sacred law then he will understand his role in bringing society into a harmonious structural whole. In other words, in the context of the perfect ashlar, the Mason can understand where his ashlar is to go in the construction of the building.

Essentially, the message of the skirret is the finding of one's purpose for the benefit of society. As in the placement of building blocks in a building, it is very important to understand where one can be of best service within society. All buildings stand because of the mutual interdependency of each of the component pieces of stonework. Each block is designed to hold particular weights and to direct particular forces. Similarly, individuals within society all have something they can offer and, through expressing this in their relationships with others, society is formed.

It is for this reason that Freemasonry is about the understanding of the Self. It is not until we understand ourselves that we can truly render ourselves extensively serviceable to mankind. Once we have understood how we can be of service, we will naturally gravitate towards the communities and areas of society we can serve most effectively.

The symbolism of the skirret doesn't just help the Freemason to find how they can be of best service to society however. This working-tool also has a more moral import. The source of the grand plan for a harmonious society is seen to be scripture, and this means that morality is implied. The closest thing to morality on a societal level is the law. It can be seen that many of society's laws have their origin at least in part in religion. In the Judaeo-Christian west, the basis of many laws can be seen to be the Ten Commandments. Therefore, if a Freemason follows the law of the land then he is perhaps naturally following the moral dictates laid down in scripture. In addition, religious scripture gives guidance on how best to behave on a more interpersonal level. For instance, Christian scripture offers guidance on forgiveness, the treatment of guests and the easing of toxic relationships between enemies.

The moral implication of the skirret is that, if everyone in society behaves morally, then we will obviously end up with an entirely moral and harmonious society.

One question that arises here is, if the volume of the sacred law represents any religion, and some religions differ in their expressions of morality, how does following the rules of one's own faith create a harmonious society?

It is true that there are many religions in the world. However, it would appear that within the core of each of these religions there is a shared moral code. For instance, murder is a sin in nearly every religion in the world, as is theft. It would appear that being human carries with it certain rules of existence, which naturally ensue. Most rules of conduct appear to serve the greater purpose of allowing people to live together in groups. We have already mentioned that human beings live together in groups to ensure survival. In fact, human beings would not perhaps have progressed very far had it not been for living in groups.

It is obvious that each human being starts their life in a very helpless state. The infant human being requires a mother to feed and nurture it, and to help it change location. The successful parenting of this mother is greatly improved by living in a group of other adult humans who can support and afford protection. The very helplessness of our beginnings requires that we live in groups. Given that each individual has a tendency to be selfish due to the survival instinct, it must follow that this selfishness must be mitigated so that group-life can function properly, and the chances of the overall survival of mankind are greatly improved.

It would seem to be clear then that wherever human beings exist there will naturally be found rules of conduct that facilitate living in groups. Therefore, every culture on Earth will have a similar set of rules to this end, and their customs and religions will naturally reflect this. Therefore, it would seem that, regardless of how many different religions there are in the world, there is a common thread of morality that binds us as human beings.

Unfortunately, it cannot be denied that there are portions of some religious scriptures that are clearly not inclusive of everyone. For instance, there is evidence in many examples of scripture in the world that certain tribes of people are meant to destroy other tribes of people. However, there is a way around this, no matter what our background traditions are. We must widen our perspectives. We should ensure that we view the entirety of the human race as a single tribe of people, and utilise the singular thread of morality that runs through all traditions of the world to govern it.

This stands to reason, especially when we consider the delicate ecosystem of the planet as a whole. We are coming to understand that we live in a finely tuned system. What changes in one place will ultimately affect another. We are therefore all at the mercy of the nature of the planet that we share. It is the responsibility of all of us to look after our own corner of the world, so that the other corners are not negatively affected along with the people who live there. We are all dependent on each other. We are all one tribe.

Consider it this way: there really is no other tribe to destroy. Any mention of destroying other humans may safely be ignored as a metaphorical warning and allegory.

It may start to seem that this book is placing a lot of emphasis on the natural evolution of morality, when Freemasonry suggests that morality is delivered from a divine source. However, the natural evolution of morality proceeds in the same way as the natural evolution of the universe, i.e. from a logical framework. Indeed, it has been found over and over again that the forces of nature follow logical rules. The need for morality to arise amongst intelligent creatures who live in a group also proceeds from logical rules. It would seem that morality emerges out of the natural logical structuring of the universe. Like everything else it proceeds from the same source that underlies and sustains everything.

Therefore, an emphasis on the natural evolution of morality in a group of individuals and the idea that the morality of scripture proceeds from a divine source are entirely compatible. Ultimately, the origin of the universe transcends human understanding, as does the 'divine' that is the subject of scripture. The underlying transcendent principles of the universe underlie everything and are within everyone, whether they are expressed scientifically or spiritually. Morality naturally evolved because of the conditions of the origin of everything, and thus was codified in many religious writings, so that everyone in human groups could be clear that this morality takes precedence over natural selfishness, for the benefit of the many.

Regardless of how the individual Freemason regards the source of morality, the ultimate lesson of the skirret is to live the most moral and helpful life one can, i.e. to serve one's fellow man so that those around us can benefit. As the individuals act in such a way, certain positive behaviours will tend to be communicated to others, who will behave similarly. By having an understanding of morality and by ensuring that they endeavour to behave in such a way as to be true to these moral standards, the general moral structure of humanity slowly improves.

Similarly, by searching within and understanding themselves sufficiently the Freemason can find how they can be of the greatest service to mankind. In this way, human society can move forward under the momentum of the individuals who comprise that society.

If everyone in society were to strive to act morally, for the benefit of others, and to improve themselves with the aim of becoming practically beneficial to others, then society would be a wonderful place indeed.

The second working-tool of the Third Degree is the pencil. This simple implement – in the context of stonework – is used by the architect of a building to draw up the plan of the intended structure. However, in the context of Freemasonry the pencil is meant to represent how our thoughts, words and actions are recorded by the Great Architect of the Universe. Once again, this states that behaviour is watched by the divine figure as represented in one's particular faith.

The implication is that the divine creator is the one who is likely to reward or punish us, and that this is the character who is recording our behaviour. Therefore, we are reminded that we should always act as if we are being watched. Generally speaking, people will never act negatively if there is someone watching, so being mindful of being watched by something or someone greater than ourselves is more likely to keep us in line wherever we are, alone or not.

Further evidence that human behaviour can be governed by the awareness of someone else watching comes from how people use the Internet. There are many examples where some people have buried people online, or expressed general opinions online, which they perhaps wouldn't ordinarily do when they were in a room with those people. The modern term for this is 'Keyboard Warrior', the idea that a person will gain confidence when they think they are not under

'The Pencil'

immediate physical threat. Since the Internet allows people to communicate over large distances without having to be actually present, those who choose to communicate in this way, which is a large percentage of the world, can choose to reinvent themselves totally.

Social networking sites can also show the natural group-policing that happens in social groups actually working. People on social networks, whilst they tend to feel more empowered to express their opinions, are very aware of the kind of public relations they might be putting out, so will tend to edit their behaviour accordingly. For example, it is very rarely that a person will place a picture of them having a rubbish time on a social networking site. Anything posted usually shows that a good time has been had at an event. Negative experiences tend not to expressed at all, unless it is of major significance where a person would like the consolation of their wider social networking group.

The idea that God is watching us is an effective psychological tool. Once again, Freemasonry acknowledges that human beings are inherently selfish creatures and have a tendency to act selfishly. Once again, it has acknowledged how groups can alter our behaviour. To be accepted in a group, one needs to continue to be seen to be following the laws of that group. If we adopt this line of thought, and throw in the idea that we are always being watched, human behaviour can be controlled so as to be more positive at all times.

Is it true that human beings need to feel they are being watched in order to be moral? It would seem that our modern society believes it to be the case. In almost every city in the world, systems of closed-circuit television have been implemented. These systems have been introduced in an attempt to ensure the security of those who might become victims in some way.

It would seem that modern humans do not believe they are being watched by an all-powerful supreme being. It seems to be true, unfortunately, that people will indeed commit crimes and atrocities when they believe they are not being watched. All over the world, houses are broken into, cars are stolen, people are attacked and murdered. These crimes are rarely committed in groups, unless those groups are complicit and don't believe they are being watched by other groups. CCTV has been installed so that people can believe they are always being watched and therefore are less likely to commit crimes.

Have the cameras been effective at reducing crime however? CCTV is only likely to work if the potential perpetrators of crimes are aware that there is a camera watching. This is why many areas protected by cameras, are accompanied by a sign that informs people of this. On many streets covered by CCTV, however, there is no sign informing people of the presence of cameras, and so crimes are still observed to be taking place on our streets despite these increased security measures.

Additionally, the apparent protection that we are afforded by surveillance has brought with it a certain sense of paranoia. There are many who are uncomfortable with the idea that their every move is watched, not because they necessarily have anything to hide, but because they view constant surveillance as something sinister. With the process of constantly being watched comes a loss of freedom. Despite being social creatures in the main, many of us value our privacy. We like the idea that we can be on our own, simply to be ourselves. We like to feel as though we are able to be free to express ourselves however we wish, and many of us feel that we can't always do this if we are always being watched.

Some of this discomfort comes from the fact that we like to feel at ease with the system of law. Despite the fact that many of our fundamental laws are based on moral codes, it can be said that other laws are not. Depending on where we live in the world there are some societal laws, which are simply unjust from a humanitarian perspective. For instance, if we live in a country where all education is banned for people below a certain economic bracket (just to produce an example from the top of my head) anyone caught on CCTV participating in illegal education is subject to punishment. Clearly, this law is unfair and needs to change, but how can anyone move to enjoy life with more educational opportunity, in this made-up situation, if people are watching so closely?

Human beings should be free to choose their own destinies, so long as certain universal moral guidelines are followed.

If the defenders of unfair laws are watching, and protecting those laws, then the chances of events like the liberation of women, for example, are less likely to be repeated, and our futures are more and more likely to be determined by faceless people who 'call the shots' and watch for those who might rebel.

All of this really supports what the pencil symbolises. If everyone acted as though they were being watched, there would be less reason to put actual surveillance in place. However, the world is far less religious than it used to be, and there is much less of a sense that we are being watched by a deity, so it is difficult for many to believe there is any real deterrent to negative behaviour, should one wish to indulge in it. In modern times, in the West, we are living in a far more atheistic society. People are less and less likely to believe in an all-seeing God. Modern times are the times of science where rationality will show the way, and not superstition. Therefore, very pragmatic approaches to policing behaviour have appeared during these times.

However, does a person really need to feel that a higher power is watching them in order to act morally in society? It doesn't seem so. Many atheists call themselves humanists, meaning that they regard human values as a general guide to morality. The moral codes that found their way into religious scripture have found their way into the behavioural guidelines of the non-religious. Once again, the natural evolution of morality holds sway. Most people will act morally in social groups and towards each other.

There are clearly times when people do not act morally and instead decide to act selfishly, but there is always a reason why people are driven to do this, whether it is desperation or mental illness.

Given the natural evolution of morality within social groups, combined with a less superstitious society, perhaps it is time to look into the faculty of the human mind that is represented by the common gavel: the force of conscience. Conscience appears to be that part of our mind that tends to keep the healthy human mind on the straight and narrow and gives us that healthy feeling of guilt if we stray from moral behaviour.

This force of conscience is perhaps the closest and most useful analogue of the all-seeing eye within modern society, and if looked at in a spiritual context is closer to that symbolised by the pencil than is at first apparent.

Firstly, it is obvious that our sense of conscience is developed at a very young age. When we first come into the world, we are only concerned with our own immediate needs, and we will get what we want in whatever way we can think of. Then, our parents tend to reprimand us when we behave in a way that is unacceptable to them. Therefore, by process of elimination, we learn which actions are good and which ones are bad. This forms a basis for our sense of conscience and, as we develop the awareness that other people are similar to us, we slowly begin to understand that others have inner lives like we do. At this stage, if we do something to another that we wouldn't like someone else to do to us, then we have the inherent understanding that this person will be made less happy, and so a healthy sense of guilt kicks in. Clearly, this is how the so-called Golden Rule came to be. The Christian idea of doing unto others as we would have them do unto us has naturally been present since human beings have been conscious. However, people do tend to forget this inherent sense of right or wrong when they give in to their perceived selfish needs.

Secondly, we must understand that the human brain developed during a long process of evolution and, therefore, the workings of the brain that have developed over time, have largely dictated how our minds work. As morality seems to naturally arise from the need for human beings to live in groups, it does necessarily follow that our natural sense of morality has developed as a consequence of the causal development of the universe over time.

Whilst this universe appears to work in ways that are made clear through scientific analysis, the further back in time we look the less clear are the initial causes of the universe we currently live in. The main obstacle to our understanding is something called the infinite regress – this is when there arises a continual need to have a cause for something we already understand. For example, imagine that we someday find the equations that explain everything about the beginning of the cosmos and how everything works from then on. One of the questions that will naturally come to mind is why does this system of equations exist? What framework allows this to happen? This would spark off a completely new search, one that, perhaps, would be resolved. However, once again, the same question would arise: what is the framework that allows this supporting framework of equations to exist?

This situation may well go on indefinitely and is therefore called the infinite regress. What this essentially means, despite all the science that will go into answering these most fundamental of questions, is that the reason why something exists, rather than nothing at all, transcends human understanding. This goes to show that transcendent things do exist, and it is not just in the lofty realms of the cosmos that this fact becomes visible. Within the realm of the human mind, there are also things which don't just temporarily defy current scientific understanding, but which may well be truly transcendent. One of these things is the problem of experience itself. Even though scientists can identify clusters of brain cells that are associated with certain types of experience, what the nature of experience actually is and how it comes about through neural impulses remains an incredibly tough problem to solve. In fact, it may never be satisfactorily solved.

However, what ensures that the universe and everything in it exists is the same thing that ensures that our sense of experience exists. This means that the transcendent cause of the universe is the transcendent cause of your mind, consciousness, and awareness, and this turns out to be very useful. Since Science is unable to lift the label on the transcendent origin of all things, even though our very being seems to rest on it, it might be possible to come into direct understanding of it in some other way that doesn't rely on reason, but instead on emotional experience and insight.

As already mentioned in this book, this is exactly why initiation is so important, but it is also why spiritual disciplines, whether provided by mainstream religious pathways or not, are so useful: they help to bring us insight. One of these insights might be that there is little difference between our naturally evolved sense of conscience and the all-seeing eye represented by the pencil. The transcendent origin of all things that some people call God is also that which makes our conscience possible. They are effectively the same thing.

The solution, then, to unravelling an understanding of the symbolism of the pencil is to realise the oneness of the transcendent with everything. The Freemason who understands this, regardless of their religious or traditional background, can safely understand that they feel the stare of the all-seeing eye whenever they pay attention to what their conscience is telling them.

In order to have a safe society that is also free from those who would watch our every move, human beings should move in the direction of becoming mindful of their own sense of conscience. Of course, how this conscience develops will partly depend on our individual upbringing. If children are brought up to think selfishly by their parents then they are more likely to be selfish when they are adults. It is the job, therefore, primarily of parents, and then teachers, to ensure that children understand more moral ways to act. The educational system can act as a safeguard against those situations where some children come from homes where they are exposed to lessons of general selfishness. Where children come from homes where decent morals are taught, on the other hand, the education system can help to reinforce this behaviour. Eventually, these children will become parents, and an overall sense of good morality will be seen to pervade civilisation.

The final working-tool in the Third Degree is the compasses. In stonework, compasses are used to measure relative proportions on building-plans, and they help in assisting the rendering of circles during the process of designing the structure. However, in Freemasonry, as may be expected, the compasses have a moral meaning. The moral lesson in this instance is that we essentially reap what we sow. The way Freemasonry puts it, is that the Great Architect of the Universe will punish or reward as the Mason obeys or disregards his divine commands.

'The Compasses'

It is possible to link this to the other two tools in the Third Degree, since it continues the theme of reminding the Freemason that they should progress through life being mindful of morality from a divine source. The compasses, however, appear to admonish the Mason that if he does not obey the moral commands of his particular faith then he will be punished by their deity.

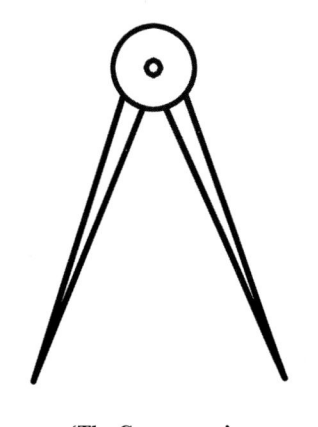

It would seem that the idea of punishment and reward is a common theme throughout all of society. The system of laws which govern each country are upheld by the idea that if a person transgresses any of them, and they are caught, that person will receive some kind of punishment.

Using punishment as a deterrent seems to derive from parental values. As has already been discussed, if a child acts in a way that doesn't meet parental approval or is caught being 'naughty', the parent will punish the child in some way, even if it is only a verbal admonishment. The idea of applying punishment after a rule has been transgressed is followed because of the very simple idea that human beings, as well as seemingly every other organism on the planet, will avoid pain and move towards sources of pleasure. This pain doesn't have to be interpreted as physical pain: it could be regarded as the emotional pain that comes from seeing that we have disappointed our parents.

The idea that we will avoid unpleasant experiences and move towards pleasant ones seems fundamental to our nervous systems. In fact, it has naturally arisen in order to ensure our survival. For example, once we have learned that fire can harm us we will automatically be mindful to be careful around any flame. Similarly, in the ancient past, once we knew there were certain types of fearsome predators to avoid, a human being would become very aware of their immediate surroundings if they were out and about. The tendency to move towards the more pleasant experiences in order to survive is heavily tied up with the idea that we feel pleasant when we have eaten, or when we are in a place where we can relax or be assured where the next meal is coming from. It would seem that the central nervous system of the human being has evolved to guide us so we are better enabled to survive.

Using this very fundamental psychological rule, human groups have found a way to utilise the selfish nature of the individual so that, paradoxically, they can curb the desire to be morally selfish. If the disobedience of any law is associated with the receipt of some kind of unpleasant experience then a person is less likely to disobey, and so the cohesive group can be maintained and order is ensured.

This very simple idea of needing the prospect of punishment in order to stay good seems a little primitive. In fact, there is still debate as to whether punitive methods to help deter criminals are at all effective. In some circles, there is the call for an alternative approach, one that comes from a place of understanding and tends to more rehabilitative methods.

If the system of law is to focus on rehabilitation, then we need to understand why it is that people commit crimes. It is not simply a case of labelling a person bad and therefore in need of punishment, and the prospect of punishment to keep this person in line. In order for the theory of rehabilitation to be effective, a human being needs to be regarded as something that can alter their behaviour and therefore act more morally in the future. This is why, in modern times, psychologists study human behaviour in order to understand root causes. Once the origin of a behaviour is understood, counter-measures can be put into place to change a person's psychology, in other words, to set up new causes for more acceptable behaviour.

This more understanding approach seems to be a far more moral approach to treating those who disobey laws, and therefore seems more progressive. In fact, it encompasses the very idea of forgiveness, a notion that can be found throughout many of the world's spiritual traditions. However, where does this leave us when we are trying to understand what the symbolism of the compasses is trying to teach us?

Perhaps, once again, we can return to the idea that there is very little difference between the nature of conscience and the source of moral conscience, which, ultimately, stems from the transcendent origin of the universe. If, as has already been suggested, we regard the personal conscience as being one with the transcendent, we can see how the compasses can be understood as a working-tool.

When we know that we have disobeyed a law, we know that we have done something wrong, and we know because our conscience creates an ever-reliable sense of guilt, whether we admit to it or not. Doing something wrong tends to play on our minds, sometimes to such a degree that we raise the level of stress in our bodies. Because of this, the physiology of a person tends to respond. It is becoming better understood that human physiology responds negatively to stress: immunity decreases, inflammatory response increases, and all sorts of ailments can ensue after long-term exposure. It is well known to most of us that there appears to be a link between stress and the onset of grey hairs, a simple example of how cells can break down due to stress in the body.

Physical response to the stress of being found out is one way in which we can see that there is something in the idea that we receive unpleasantness from being immoral. Generally, those who feel they haven't broken any rules tend to feel that life runs very smoothly and tend to be happier, so long as the conditions for happiness are there. Clearly, then, these pleasant experiences can be seen to emerge as a natural consequence of behaving morally.

Moving away from the idea that acting immorally can generate stress, there is also the point that a life of selfishness and immorality towards others tends to have its own natural and external results. People will gravitate less towards people who act immorally. Those who will cluster around an immoral individual tend to be other individuals who are themselves immoral. This situation alone is not conducive to a happy life, as there can be no real foundation of trust. Therefore true and rewarding relationships of any kind are difficult to form, whereas a warm, less selfish person will attract a greater variety of people and benefit from the relationships that can be created, ensuring the human need to form strong bonds with groups, and increasing their happiness level.

Living any life of immorality and selfishness, even if it is somehow lived entirely guilt-free, seems to only eventually result in an unfulfilling and unhappy life. It would seem that nature does indeed punish or reward as we act selfishly or selflessly.

This, then, would seem to nicely resolve the lesson of the compasses. The source of all things does indeed seem to have ensured that punishment or reward is written into the very workings of the cosmos, and that they become apparent through the logic of human existence itself.

As well as teaching a moral lesson, something else is alluded to by the compasses. It is well known that compasses are directly related to the construction of circles. However, what may not be so widely known is the fact that the circle is directly related to matters of spirituality in many cultures around the world. This is because the heavens themselves appear to be replete with circles. The sun appears to be a circle, as does the moon. The sun rises in the east and sets in the west, apparently completing a circular path each day. The years are constructed from a repeating cycle of four seasons. Everywhere human beings can look in the heavens, circles are to be found.

In the many cultures of the world, the realm of the divine is in the heavens above and so, naturally, the circle has been logically linked to all things divine. The universe itself has even been described as a circle where the centre is everywhere and the circumference nowhere, and the idea that the universe is infinite in terms of time and space is often represented as the *ouroboros*, the serpent that is bent into a circle, eating its own tail.

One of the most beautiful ways of thinking of the transcendent reality behind the cosmos can be illustrated by the circle. If the centre of the circle is seen to be the source of all things, and the circumference is the progression of time, then it can be seen that, no matter where one is on the circumference, the centre appears ever-present, unchanged, and at right-angles to the path of the outer edge. From the point of view of the centre of the circle, all of time is experienced at once as it encircles it. In this way, we can see that an all-pervasive transcendent and unchanging origin is described along with the ever-changing march of time.

Notice that the example of the circle providing insight into the relationship with the divine also mentions the right angle. As we are already aware, the right angle is the angle of the square, and so we can perhaps begin to see why the two symbols of the square and compasses are used to denote Freemasonry as a Society.

The compasses, being the tool of the traditional stonemason most closely related to the circle, are clearly the ideal symbol to represent the cycle of the universe processing around the circle. However, when combined with the square, in other words when using the right angle, the source of the circle, the centre, may be discovered. This view of the compasses working alongside the square to reveal the deeper underlying truth of the cosmos directly aligns with Freemasonry as an expression of the ancient idea of initiation. Remembering that the purpose of initiation is to reveal inner truths about the Self and the universe, and to unveil their interconnectedness the Freemason uses the square and compasses as they journey on their path of esoteric knowledge.

Once the centre of the circle, as a symbol for the source of all things, is revealed to the Freemason, they will then be able to see the greater importance of the compasses for, if one were to place one point of the compasses onto the centre, one could describe a circle with the other point. This clearly points to the process of the creation of all things. Therefore, as the Freemason progresses on their journey, they come to understand the relationship between the origin and everything else in the cosmos. To show that this knowledge is developing, at the beginning of the journey, in the combined symbol of the square and compasses, the points of the compasses are hidden by the square. However, by the time the Freemason arrives at the Third Degree, both compass points are revealed. This shows that the true relationship between existence and the transcendent source is buried beneath the material of the universe, as represented by the square, yet can be revealed by studious inquiry.

As has been mentioned, the square is often seen to represent the Earthly domain, and everything in it. The Earth is metaphorically said to have four corners. Therefore another interpretation of the combined square and compasses utilises the idea that the human being is a combination of Earthly material and divine spirit. As a Freemason progresses on their journey, the legs of the compasses are slowly revealed to show that the spiritual part of the human being is shining through and has taken control of the baser material represented by the square. Seeing the use of the compasses alongside the square in this way, but combined with the above interpretation of wider significance, points the Freemason towards the idea that the source of the Self and the source of the universe are, in fact, one.

Looking at the square and compasses combination in yet another way, we can see that the human morality represented by the square has been placed under direct influence of a more stable morality derived from the transcendent source of all things. This makes sense when seen in the context of the other tools in the Third Degree. Both the pencil and the skirret seem to be directing the Freemason to turn their attention to understanding divine morality by understanding how it is laid down in their own expression of the Volume of the Sacred Law. As a transcendent law is revealed through spiritual discipline and study, the Freemason is better enabled to express this in their daily life and may allow their behaviour to change for the benefit of society. Hence, the symbolism of the spiritually related compasses overshadowing the square.

Still another yet related way that the compasses can be interpreted is the idea of keeping in due bounds with all mankind. In this interpretation, the square represents the morality of the individual Mason while the overshadowing compasses represent the general morality and laws of mankind. This interpretation helps to put to rest the idea that Freemasonry is a secret society that is in danger of following its own agenda; the Masonic ceremonies themselves imply that Freemasons are to keep themselves in due bounds with all humanity.

As well as a tool to convey the lesson of morality, the compasses are clearly incredibly important on the journey of the Freemason and help them to uncover their relative place in the wider universe. Looking back over all of the tools of the Third Degree, they are all about the overall plan of the building work in building terms. Therefore, they symbolise the wider perspective of a Freemason's place in the universe, once they have crafted themselves into a more serviceable state.

Effectively, the tools of the Third Degree create an overall context for the tools of the previous two Degrees. As has been already mentioned, the crafting of the First Degree, aided by the guiding self-measurement of the tools of the Second Degree, are all in order to prepare the Freemason for service in the wider world. This mirrors the actual working of a stone. The material is worked on and crafted, helped by the tools of measurement, in order to render the stone serviceable for the structure for which it is intended.

As the Freemason progresses through their Masonic life, they pay attention to all of the faculties intended for development through the contemplative Masonic life. In the First Degree, the Freemason is taught how best to utilise the 24 hours they are given each day. As they progress through their days they are encouraged to listen to the voice of conscience, which is a guiding light within, that will help point them in the right moral direction. In order to be more serviceable, Freemasons are encouraged to educate themselves as much about the world in as many subjects as they can, and to educate themselves specifically about their own particular area of specialism in life, whatever it might be, so that they can offer the best service possible in their work.

In the Second Degree, the emphasis is on being mindful of where work still needs to be done. Therefore the Freemason is expected to constantly be aware of whether they are acting completely morally with other people and when they are not, to ensure they focus more on their conscience and education of how best to relate to others. The Freemason is invited to be mindful of whether their actions are based on a sense of equality with others and, if not, to alter it through conscience and education. Finally, for the Second Degree, the Freemason is encouraged to test whether their actions are always matched to the most upright of their intentions.

Ultimately, in the Third Degree, the Freemason is encouraged to seek out the best way to place themselves in society so that they can be of best use to mankind, and they are taught to ensure that the highest and most general moral rules dictate their behaviour. Alongside all of this, the Freemason seeks to uncover the relationship between the source of all things and the emergent cosmos.

The final product after the working-tools of Freemasonry have worked on the Mason is the smooth ashlar, and it is this symbol to which we turn in the next chapter.

CHAPTER 6

THE PERFECT ASHLAR

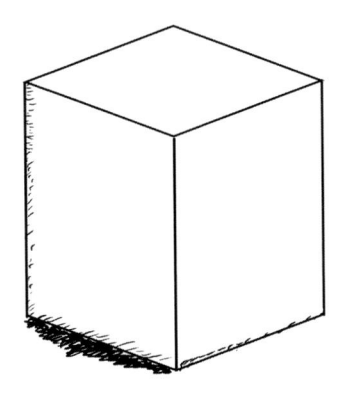

'A Perfect Ashlar'

After the Freemason has progressed through the three Degrees of Craft Freemasonry they have been introduced to the symbols representing the various faculties of which they must make mindful use in order to craft the person that they once were, represented by the rough ashlar, into the morally more refined version of themselves represented by the smooth or perfect ashlar.

A perfect ashlar in stone-masonry is a stone block, which has been crafted by skilled masons, into a more usable form as an element of the intended superstructure of which it is to become a part. Once the stone has been hewn from rock in the quarry, then transported to the building site, it is the job of the apprentice to begin to craft the stone from its natural form into one that resembles what it is to become. This is where the First Degree of Freemasonry, the Entered Apprentice Degree, gets its name. As has been explained, the tools of an apprentice comprise the gauge or ruler, the common gavel and the chisel. The apprentice is to work with these tools until the stone is ready to be passed to a more skilled workman, known as a craftsman. Obviously, by the time the Entered Apprentice has finished working on the rough ashlar, it is far from complete and is still unready for inclusion into the building.

After the apprentice has worked on the stone it is passed to the skilled craftsman for further work and honing. The end-result of this stage of the work will be the perfect ashlar that is ready to be included into the construction of the building. Similarly, to the Entered Apprentice Degree, the Second Degree in Freemasonry takes its name from this operative phase of stonework, and is called the Degree of a Fellow Craft.

The craftsman works with the same tools as the apprentice, with the addition of some other tools of measurement, which include the square, the level, and the plumb rule. As the craftsman further smooths and prepares the stone for the building, they are constantly measuring it in order to ensure its transformation into the desired form. The square tells them that the edges and corners of the developing ashlar are moving closer and closer to the desired ninety-degree angle, while the level informs them that its surface is perfectly flat and that the block stands level with respect to the ground, so that it will form a proper upright structure once it is put in place. The plumb rule, similarly, shows that the ashlar is upright on all sides and so, once again, fit for its purpose in the construction of an upright structure. These tools will also be used in the general construction of the intended building.

The craftsman will also use their skill to carve the stone with particular patterns which might further beautify the intended structure. This requires a knowledge of the intended overall design of the final edifice so that patterns can be continued on similar, adjacent stone blocks. This awareness of the overall design comes from the more senior craftsman on the building site, the master mason.

Master masons in the context of a building site, besides lending their skills to the crafting of the stone, act as foremen to the other stonemasons; it is they who are in close contact with the building's architect and it is therefore their job to ensure the design is realised accurately. Once again, the Third Degree in Freemasonry takes its name from this phase of the crafting process, and so is called the Degree of a Master Mason.

Here, as has been explained, there are particular tools associated with the master mason's work, namely the skirret, pencil, and compasses. The skirret enables the master mason to lay out the ground on which the building will be constructed, all according to the plan, which has been created by the building's architect. In order to create that plan, a skilled architect has utilised, along with other tools, the pencil to draw the intended structure. The compasses help to determine the various sizes and proportions, so that the entire building can be scaled up and represented accurately on the actual ground.

As has already been seen, each of these stages of operative stone-masonry has its analogue in the different Degrees of Speculative Masonry, or Freemasonry. However, instead of working on actual stone blocks, the material being worked on is the inner material of the individual Masonic Initiate. As they move through the allegorical Degrees the Freemason moves closer to the Degree of a Master Mason, one who has mastered the science of self-crafting, working towards the great secret of the Self.

The job of the master mason, incidentally, is to liaise with the building's architect, which also has its analogue in the world of the Master Freemason. He has come to understand that in this case the architect is the architect of the world and the universe. In the final chapter of this book, we shall explain in more detail the nature of the secret of a Master Mason in Freemasonry, a secret that, once found, is incommunicable, and which only reveals itself to those who have made the necessary efforts to uncover it.

The perfect ashlar in the speculative Craft of Freemasonry therefore represents the human being who has mastered the Self. Being at the other end of the journey of Freemasonry, the perfect ashlar stands as the complete opposite of the rough ashlar, which represents the person just entering Freemasonry. Mindful use of the symbolic tools has given the Master Mason mastery over the various faculties comprising human nature. What description of the Freemason as represented by the perfect ashlar will therefore enable us to fully understand this symbol?

The first thing the true Master Mason has mastered is effective utilisation of their time. Having passed through the Degrees of Freemasonry the importance of time has been thoroughly driven home. Initially, their lesson came from the twenty-four inch gauge, which taught that, ideally, the Freemason should divide their day into different activities.

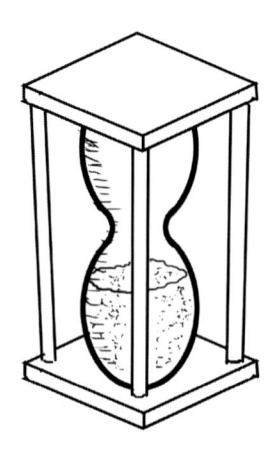

'A Master Mason Effectively Uses Their Time'

Most of us, of course, do this. We spend around eight hours each day at work, rendering service in return for payment or reward. The exertion spent at our work is hopefully nullified when we refresh ourselves with rest and leisure time, this being very important if we are to remain healthy. However, the twenty-four inch gauge suggests yet another thing that we should pay attention to, and that is the subject of spirituality.

It can be said we are now living in what is becoming more and more of a post-religious society. There are more people in the world today who would call themselves either atheist or agnostic, as a result of which the churches are slowly losing their congregations. Nowadays, the world seems satisfied that science will solve our existential as well as our practical problems.

Unfortunately, this may not be so. Whilst it is possible that science will one day understand the intricate workings of the vast material universe and, potentially, in the distant future, even enable us to create a universe of our own in the laboratory, this will only tell us about the material universe and how it works. It does nothing to explain how there comes to be something other than nothing. The answer to that question lies beyond the material realm and, perhaps, will never be viewed by the gaze of reason and scientific method.

Therefore, if society drifts too far from the possibilities of the spiritual as pertaining to the underlying reality of all things it may be so comforted and dazzled by the possibilities of empirical science that it takes a huge step backwards without even knowing it,.

Of course, one of the things that have turned people away from the subject of spirituality is the terrible atrocities committed in the name of religion. There are even atrocities written in the text of the holy scriptures of these religions: hardly enlightened behaviour! However, if the scriptures of religion are seen as allegorical, containing deep spiritual truths, then the terrible things written become the same as the terrible things expressed in works of recognised fiction. The atrocities are used to comment on and drive home deeper messages about the spiritual core of humankind.

Freemasonry drives home the importance of regaining spiritual insights, as will be discussed later in this book and it hopes to achieve this through the process of initiation.

As well as having found a balance between work, leisure, and attending to spiritual matters, the Master Mason also turns his attention to how he can help other people in the wider community. They do this by rendering service and aid to all who seek it, and embrace the opportunity and undertake it cheerfully, understanding that, as a member of society, they are part of an interconnected network that is dependent on the mutual support of its individual parts.

The importance of time is also driven home to the Master Mason by an awareness of the temporary nature of human existence. The very fact a person is not around for long in the grand scheme of things implies they should act immediately in being of service, rather than resting on their laurels.

As the Master Mason moves through their days, using their time productively and rewardingly on the different levels, they are also equipped with a refined sense of conscience. This force of conscience is something that appears to be innate within the organism of the human being. From a very young age, we quickly acquire knowledge of what is right and what is wrong. Also, quite early on, we become aware that the people around us are similar to us in their general inner make-up. We may not understand exactly how this comes about, but we certainly have a sense of this truth.

Whenever we are tempted to do something that might be considered morally wrong, there is always something within us telling us we perhaps shouldn't follow up on this action. The deciding factor when choosing whether or not to undertake such behaviour usually comes down to selfishness. If the action can be seen to be of benefit to us, and the resolve to not behave in this way remains weak, we will disregard the inner voice and act in a manner unbecoming a moral human.

A very simple example of this is being in a queue at a cash machine. It becomes your turn to go up to the machine but, as you step up to it, you notice a twenty-pound note sticking out of it. The person before you is still in sight. Now, imagine that you are short of money; this extra twenty-pound note will benefit you immensely. Here is the dilemma: do you take the twenty-pound note and keep it, or do you shout after the person who has just walked away to give him the money that is rightfully theirs. Deep within, there is probably the urge to give the money to the correct person, but then there is also the fact that you are short of money.

This perfectly illustrates the kind of situation where a heightened sense of conscience determines behaviour. For the Freemason the only action to take, regardless of personal circumstance, would be to call after the person who left the money. This is because the Freemason has pledged to live their lives by the highest of moral virtues as a kind of overarching prime directive. The Freemason must always favour the morally correct action.

This is very powerful, as with continued use this resolve to act morally, regardless of circumstances, helps the baser impulses to die away. Listening to the guidance of conscience helps to move the psychology of a person from the animalistic and the primal to something grander and more purposeful. It also does the job of putting the person in contact with the core of his being, which, as has been mentioned, contains the genuine secrets of the Master Mason, and indeed of life itself.

In order to aid the Freemason in their daily life they commit themselves to the very valuable faculty of education. Many of the problems of mankind are based on ignorance. Where there is insufficient learning, superstition creeps in, and this usually leads to human error.

To learn about the world then is something that human beings must endeavour to do. If it wasn't for the progress made in the sciences, for instance, many of the things we take for granted in the modern world would not exist. Imagine, for example, that penicillin had never been discovered. How many people from the time of its discovery would have died? Clearly, without the human endeavour to learn, there can be no progress, and there can be no improvement in conditions and comfort.

It has been said that progress is not always a good thing. However, this is patently not true. All human progress, where it is genuine, is a good thing; it is merely the methods by which we achieve such progress which lead to the conclusion that some progress is bad.

The clearest example of this is how industry developed and, in some cases is still developing, with complete disregard for the surrounding environment. The damage that has been caused can, in some measure, be forgiven because it has been due to ignorance. In the days of the Industrial Revolution, the fact that human affairs were so bound up with the health of the world was, in the main, lost on the people of the time. This clearly illustrates that there was a need to understand such interdependency, which would have required scientific study and education.

Nowadays, in some areas, there is the awareness that human activity is affecting the world at large, and thankfully, measures are slowly being put into place that will harmonise with the positive health of the natural world.

Ignorance has had its effects everywhere. In the days when the slave trade was rife all across the world (and, in some parts, still is) differences of race were a convenient excuse for accepting ignorance over the obvious truth, which was staring them in the face: all in the name of cheap labour.

In stone-masonry, the chisel is nearly always used in conjunction with the common gavel. In Freemasonry, this implies that education should always be guided by the force of conscience. If this policy is maintained, then human progress will be assured and will always take into account the side effects of such progress so that work can be done to mitigate them.

Finally on the subject of education, in many places around the word there are systems of enforced ignorance. In these places, people are denied an education, which could be of such great benefit both to the individual and to their society as a whole. It is clear then that in order for progress to be made, this kind of behaviour should be stopped. It is only through the education of everyone that peace will eventually reign and the world solve a lot of its problems.

As has been already covered in the explanation of a Freemason's use of a heightened sense of conscience, the Freemason is committed to acting according to the highest moral principles, regardless of anything else. Of course, it is important for the Freemason to discern what the best moral actions actually are. In order to do this, the Master Mason has perfected the use of the Golden Rule as a guide to their actions. The Golden Rule, as has been explained previously, can be summed up in the statement that a person should do to others as they would have done to themselves. This is also known as Square Conduct.

In the dealings that a person has in their day-to-day lives it is always important to understand the best way to act. Of course, primarily this is guided by the force of conscience that speaks from within. As the Freemason interacts with other people in this manner, they find that people are more likely to act in the same way in their dealings with them.

The lesson of the square in the Second Degree is that it represents the material world, and that the rules we work with in society generally have their origin in society. However, it is important to note that the use of conscience can be considered to come from a purer source and will dictate the correct thing to do with regard to other people.

A good example of this is if a country makes it law not to educate women, or people with a lower income. This law can safely be said to come from human beings. Remember, the dual meaning of the square is Square Conduct and the representation of human morality. The refusal to educate people as a law can clearly be seen to be wrong from a more enlightened perspective. Looking at such a law whilst listening to the voice of conscience inspires the feeling that there is an injustice being done here which needs to be dealt with. This feeling arises from a deeper source, one that is clearly aware of more general and purer principles of morality. Sometimes, then, the laws of man are inferior to the laws suggested by principles of human equality which should always be adhered to.

Here, the subject of equality has naturally arisen in the discussion of the symbol of the Master Mason, who is represented by the perfect ashlar. A heightened sense of natural equality is a characteristic of the fully initiated Freemason.

Once again, this natural sense of equality is guided by the combined forces of conscience and education. The most important thing to be educated about, in this regard, is the Self. To understand the inner workings of the Self is to understand others, despite the wide variety of differences that are apparent in the world.

The Master Mason understands that there lies within a certain spirit that craves expression, despite the mortal frame in which we find ourselves. An obvious indicator of this, which has been discussed previously, is the resolve of the differently abled human being to overcome the obstacles of their material nature and to achieve more. Despite the apparent differences, people faced with such challenges feel the urge to ignore them and find a way to achieve great things. Stories of such endeavours are truly inspiring, and are testament to the existence of a higher human spirit.

The human spirit has been documented in many other areas too. Wherever human beings have overcome their natural obstacles in favour of achievement, the evidence of the human spirit can be found. Examples of this include people like Christopher Columbus who, regardless of the fact that no one knew what lay across the sea, nevertheless journeyed across and would eventually, albeit accidentally, discover the American continent. The journey into space is a result of human beings defying the natural limitations of gravity to explore the skies above.

The Freemason, then, seeing evidence of such a human spirit everywhere, understands that there is commonality between all human beings, and between other human beings and themselves. Therefore, the Master Mason strives to act according to what they know connects every member of mankind, regardless of circumstances. Armed with this key knowledge they will act with equanimity, and cheerfully embrace the opportunity to aid other human beings, realise their potential, and teach them that circumstances of perceived limitation are illusory when compared with the potential of the human spirit.

In upholding moral codes and seeking to maintain a sense of equality, the ideal Freemason must commit themselves to always remaining upright in their conduct.

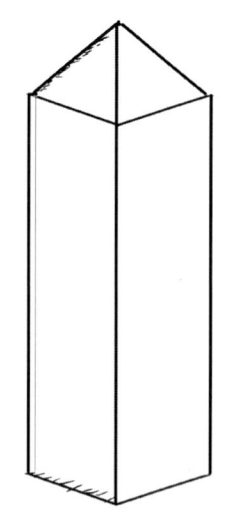

'An Upright Structure, Indicating the Upright Mason'

The term 'upright' refers back to the idea that a structure that is upright is effectively pointing at the heavens. The structure, in this state, can then be seen to be a symbol of reaching for the highest plane of virtue and morality. However, such structures are constantly battling against the pull of gravity. In order to defy gravity, a structure should be perfectly erect, with no give on any side, where gravity might be given the advantage.

To remain morally upright then involves a similar battle against the baser nature. It is as if the temptation to act according to our lower natures, is a constant force exerting its influence to pull the Master Mason from the higher morality to which they aspire. However, as has been mentioned, thanks to the human spirit and its drive to defy actual gravity for the exploration of space, this same human spirit can exert a powerful counterbalancing to the force that would pull us down.

The idea of maintaining moral behaviour, as informed by the conscience, regardless of the situation or perceived benefit of alternative behaviour speaks of a refined will. Through the sheer power of human will, the human being can soar to heights of morality and truly defy the constant call of their primitive natures.

All the moral development that a Freemason undertakes through the process of initiation and the contemplation that follows is placed in the wider context of society. Since the ideal Master Mason is symbolised by the perfect ashlar, which is ready to go into the construction of the wider building design, it naturally follows that they will be prepared to interact with other elements, realised as other members of society.

It has already been thoroughly explained that the realisation of the interconnectedness of the whole of society and, in fact, the world, is the goal of the Freemason. It is the realisation of this interdependency, which brings to light the natural realisation that they can be of greater service.

In Freemasonry, the true nature of this interdependency can be realised by coming to terms with the principles of morality, which are outlined within the pages of spiritual scripture and texts. All of the holy texts of the world are inspired by the deep sense of the transcendent reality, which acts as the basis for the intangible human spirit. Therefore, Freemasonry implies that the way to experience this reality in our core, to its fullest, is to study the texts that have been so inspired. It is only then that the secret of ourselves, which we share with all humankind, can reveal where we can be most effectively placed to the benefit of society.

As well as the moral development, which has been thoroughly explored, there are other parts of human nature that must be wrestled with if the will of the Freemason is to gain full control of their inner Self. The most dominant of these parts is the gamut of emotions to which we are all subject.

The emotional world of the human being is really the ground of human experience and reality. Without emotions, we would be unable to enjoy a beautiful sunset, or the wonders of nature, or the touch of someone dear to us. It is emotion that truly colours our world. Yet, these are all positive emotions. Of course, there are also the negative emotions and, because we are so influenced by emotion, they are also the reason why there is so much ugliness in the world.

The ideal Master Mason then has perfect control of their emotions. They are able to stand guard and allow the positive emotions to pass unhindered into their awareness, but also to halt and question the negative emotions that will also arise from time to time. The end-goal of this is to ensure that the behaviour of the Freemason is not influenced by negative emotions, which can lead to ugliness and damage to themselves and those around them.

To help them in this task, the ideal Master Mason has realised that all negative emotion has at its source just one primary negative emotion: the emotion of fear. Fear is incredibly powerful and has developed to assist us in our survival. If we were unable to feel fear, then we would boldly step into dangerous situations which would eventually spell certain doom for us and, if no one could feel fear, for the rest of humanity.

Fear works by two mechanisms: fight or flight. This means that if we perceive a potentially threatening situation we are given a choice. Most who are presented with such threats choose to flee, because fighting can cause further damage and is itself a threat to health and survival. However, if a way of escape is not clear, then the instinct to fight prevails.

In order to fight a threat, another emotion arises that is usually known as hate: this involves directing one's attention towards the threat in preparation for battle. It is therefore important, when studying the subject of human emotions, to understand that whenever we feel hatred it is as the result of fear and of not having been allowed to propel ourselves away from the perceived danger.

A simple example of hatred is often felt in the workplace. The words, 'I hate my boss', have often been said in all walks of working life. However, it is important to analyse the cause of this hatred, and to better understand how that negative emotion works. Furthermore, it should be assumed here, for the purposes of simplicity, that the boss in question is a relatively decent person. How then, could this hatred arise?

Much of the cause of this hatred comes from the fact that many people go to work because they feel they have to, usually because they need to earn money for the survival of themselves and their family. Much of the time, therefore, a person will be guided by the need to acquire money rather than feeling at leisure to find a job that they truly enjoy.

Because of this, this person in the workplace will do their best at work, but might secretly resent having to come to work in the first place when they could be doing something else.

Now, usually, it is the job of a person in a position of authority to ensure that the quality of work being done is of a high standard. It is also the boss's job to give out work to people, despite how much they already have. Therefore, quite naturally, the boss becomes a person that the worker's psychology has a tendency to fear. Also, the worker feels that they need this job and so don't feel they are in a position to flee from this perceived threat. The only recourse left for the worker's emotional make-up is then the fight response, which fuels a certain degree of hatred.

This kind of reactionary hatred can be seen all across society throughout the world, and is often directed against authority-figures. Even the perception of government can be fuelled by a degree of proclaimed hatred, even if that government is relatively benevolent. Again, this comes from the fact that members of society are well aware that it is the government that decides on the course that the country is taking and that this is a situation they feel unable to flee from. They therefore have a sense of fear that they might not be able to rely on those in charge to decide on the best courses of action to guide society, which might impact them.

Regardless of the source of hatred, it can clearly be seen that its source comes from the fight or flight mechanisms of fear. However, if the Freemason is to prevent hatred from affecting their behaviour negatively, how are they to avoid this perfectly natural, psychological reaction? The answer is through understanding and the ability to work in harmony with others.

In the case of the hatred towards one's boss at work, the ideal Freemason has learned how to defuse such hatred. The Freemason, being a student of human nature, understands that the boss is only doing their job and, much of the time, would probably rather not be in the position of having to put pressure on people. The ideal Freemason also embraces the workplace as an opportunity to be of the best service to the community. They will therefore endeavour to perform their tasks to the very best of their ability, and may even strive to provide more service than is expected of them. By doing this, they automatically have no reason to fear the boss; because that boss will always observe that the Freemason is performing well. In fact, rendering more service than is usually expected is often a way of gaining promotion and improving circumstances for oneself. This is not the primary reason for providing the best service, though. That lies in the dedication to provide service.

Since, in this particular scenario, there is no need to fear the boss, the flight instinct is short-circuited and so the possibility of hatred is defused. Indeed, rather than feeling hatred, the true Master Mason is driven by the opposing feeling of love. In their dedication to providing the best service for others it is implied that they are behaving selflessly, which is the outcome of the purest kind of love. Therefore, it is by providing active and selfless service to others that we counteract the predisposition to negative emotion.

Also, if the source of hatred is fear then faith must be a contributing factor to its opposite. As the Freemason strives to be selfless, a certain degree of faith arises in the beneficial outcomes of such behaviour, as the safety inherent in faith dispels the fear of the inherent unknown in life and the Freemason becomes happier.

A facet of the human animal that is also driven by fear is the tendency towards greed and therefore excess. To obtain more than one's immediate needs is a way of counteracting the perceived threat of running out of resources in the future. Unfortunately, such behaviour has a tendency to deprive other people of what they might need. This is a situation which can be observed throughout the world. A classic way of expressing the discrepancy that is seen all around us is the fact that eighty percent of the world's wealth is in the hands of twenty percent of the world's population.

The driving force behind this has already been explained. It is the natural inclination of a human being's more primitive nature to accumulate resources. Furthermore, some people in the world are naturally very good at accumulating such resources. Even when they seem to have more than enough, the natural impulse to obtain more is still a driving factor.

Thankfully, some of the richest people in the world have shown evidence of feeling an embarrassment of riches and have begun to take heed of the great responsibility that has been laid upon them: that they should use their amassed wealth to give back to society and improve global conditions.

From the Masonic point of view, this responsibility is driven home throughout the process of initiation and as the Freemason pursues the Masonic life. The call that Freemasonry makes to every Freemason's heart is the call to give charitably whenever they can. The implication here is that the resources of the world are to be shared amongst humanity and, as the Freemason amasses advantages of any kind in whatever measure, they should feel the responsibility to utilise the ability that such an advantage gives them for the benefit of the rest of society and the world.

The true Master Mason, therefore, controls the apparent predisposition to excess, as they understand that to obtain more than is needed comes from a position of fear and not faith. Through continued education and contemplation, the Freemason appreciates there is plenty in the world to go around were it not for the fear of mankind blocking its beneficial distribution.

Of course, the sense of service to others that a Freemason is encouraged to feel is expressed through an innate sense of purpose, in that there is something which the Freemason can do in their lives that can truly benefit society.

The sense of inner purpose stands opposed to the idea that a human being must find work for the express purpose of earning money. The Mason that is represented by the perfect ashlar is driven to express their unique gifts. Yet, in order to find these gifts, the Freemason sometimes needs to look deep within and truly understand themselves.

Thankfully, this is the very idea of initiation. As the Freemason contemplates the symbols they come across in the various ceremonies of their initiation, their inward gaze begins to highlight who they are. After all, it is sometimes very difficult to truly know ourselves when we are faced with the demands of the external world. It is all too easy to make every twist and turn in response to what our lives demand, and to be purely reactive. In this confusion of activity, human beings typically believe that this defines who they are. Of course, who we are runs much deeper than the external world allows us to see.

If a person takes some time to step back from the demands of the world and looks within, light can slowly be shed on who they are. Given time, the true preferences, likes and dislikes can rise to the surface and, sometimes, the person thus revealed in conscious awareness can come as a complete surprise. It is at this point that a human being can become aware of particular passions they might have for particular activities, or lines of work.

When an individual feels the tug of a particular passion, it is that person's inner core expressing a desire that has been, as yet, unfulfilled. Many people feel this passion, yet ignore it because of the perceived external demands. However, it is possible to develop outlets of these favoured lines of service and expression whilst still managing the demands of ordinary life. As more and more energy is put into creating ways of true personal expression, one then finds that it can become the main outlet of service.

If a person is passionate about doing something, then they are likely to truly enjoy performing the service, not because of the financial reward they receive, but because of the emotional satisfaction such expression always provides. This is key to rendering the best service possible to others: to feel amazing about providing that service.

One of the main oppositions to the inward development of any human being is their sense of ego. The ego arises in most human beings and is a result of identification with the illusion that there is a separate Self that stands apart from everyone else. It is in this state that fear arises, because the person who feels separate feels in some way alone and cut off from the rest of the world, and that it is up to them to maintain their survival. Therefore, the ego arises as a natural instinct to preserve oneself and to survive.

However, through the revelation that human beings do not work alone in any endeavour, the Freemason begins to feel they are not separate and that they are in fact part of the cohesive whole of society, with their own particular contributions to offer. Rather than supporting merely the progress of the Self, fuelled by a sense of ego, the true Master Mason sees that their happiness and survival depends on feeling part of a community.

Once a person has opened up to the wider community, they tend to realise, as is taught to the Freemason, that they have been reliant on others for a very long time. In fact, they become consciously aware that they would not have even been able to survive without the intervention of other people, and that this has been true ever since they first came into this world. The ego, at this point, becomes meaningless, and it loses its power to influence behaviour.

The removal of the power of the ego is imperative in the modern world, which appears to be obsessed with it. All around us there are examples of what can only be regarded as ego worship. This has never been more apparent than in the media. The world, it seems, is obsessed with celebrity and the enjoyment of fame and fortune. In fact, it is a driving force for many people, particularly the young, to pursue fame.

However, the truth of the end-result of aggrandising the ego and becoming famous is far from that which is advertised via the various channels of media. Fame is in fact a trap to many who have attained it. Imagine being so famous that you can't even walk out of your house without being spotted by people who want to come over to you and be a part of your life for a few moments. Imagine being so harassed by people that you have to hire security guards to form a barrier between yourself and other human beings. Imagine having to secure your house from the infiltration by those who might wish to earn money simply by getting a picture of you.

The paranoia, fear and sense of isolation that inevitably arises from a lifestyle like this can become too much to bear. Historically, the newspapers have been filled with cases of celebrities who have turned to substance abuse to help them psychologically flee from the imprisonment and misery their lives have become. Going back to the idea that the sense of fear works with the mechanisms of fight or flight, the fear of the world which grows within some famous people often turns to hate because they can't seem to escape the effects of being well known. This hatred becomes self-hatred and a hatred of life which, unfortunately, can sometimes end tragically.

However, the media carries on extolling fame as if it is something to aim for. Therefore, people need to educate themselves and realise what fame really is.

The promotion of the ego can be dangerous for healthy human development even when it is not attached to fame. When a person is constantly advertising how good they are at a particular thing, or gives off vibes that they are somehow superior, other human beings tend to treat this person with contempt and even avoid them. The sad thing about this is that it is fear that is causing the individual to feel the need to constantly advertise themselves in such a way. This fear stems from the fact that, deep down, they perhaps don't feel they are recognised as being of any use to the people around them, and that people will not notice them unless they force upon them what it is they want them to see.

The natural antidote to this is to actively promote usefulness in any endeavour. With sustained effort, these endeavours will bear fruit in the form of the realisation that they are useful, regardless of whether people recognise it or not. Again, as a result of this, the emphasis on the ego melts away.

Throughout the journey of the Freemason, it can sometimes be mistakenly believed that the state represented by the perfect ashlar is an end-goal to aim for and, once it is achieved, there will be no more work to be undertaken. Unfortunately, this is a mistaken view; in most cases, the job of the Freemason is ongoing throughout all of their lives.

The human being is a fragile animal, with the world constantly throwing new challenges at them. As the Freemason moves through the unfolding of their own life there is a variety of experiences, and not all of them are good. Whenever life throws a challenging time at us, it is necessarily met with a reaction fuelled by the basic drives that have come pre-packaged in our lineage as human beings.

The primitive aspects of ourselves are incredibly powerful, and rightly so. In the times before our modern society developed, human beings lived a lot closer to nature, and danger was all around. Life was spent, as all wild animals spend their lives, on the brink of starvation and under the constant fear that life might be snatched away in a moment by some predator.

At that point in human history, we needed our emotional and instinctive wits in order to survive. Since everyone lived in this way, the order of the day was to look after one's own and oneself, regardless of other people. Therefore, if a human being saw that another had some food and they were finding it difficult to gain any for themselves, the situation might occur where violence would erupt with an end-goal of obtaining the food. The needs of anyone beyond the immediate family or tribe were not necessarily in the forefront of most people's minds.

These days, then, we can be forgiven when the hard work we have undertaken to live to the highest possible standards is let down by the re-emergence of selfish needs and desires. Unfortunately, human physical evolution hasn't caught up with the moralistic ideals of modern humans. We are in an almost constant struggle with the genetic programming passed down to us by our ancestors. Therefore, to regard the perfect ashlar as a pinnacle end-point would necessitate finding some way of dispelling the effects of genetic programming.

Similarly, a person who is interested in Freemasonry and who has studied enough of what its intentions are might be led to believe that the initiation process itself might have the effect of creating change, simply by undergoing it. This, of course, is an error.

Initiation is meant to be a springboard from which future contemplation can grow. It can truly be said that it is not in the lodge room where a Freemason sees the bulk of their development happen. It is, instead, out in the world of ordinary life that changes are observed.

Only by paying attention to what the ceremonies of initiation have to say about the symbols which are presented and then attempting to further understand the meaning alluded to can a Freemason then try out the lessons in the laboratory of their own lives. Sometimes, the Freemason will believe they understand the meaning of some symbol or another and, as the experience of life progresses, suddenly find that they were mistaken.

The smooth ashlar is intended as an ideal to work towards. This being the case, it is unlikely that any one Freemason will ever achieve the lofty standards represented by this smooth stone. However, it is important to understand that having the ideal to work towards, even if one knows that it can never be fully achieved, is incredibly important.

As a simple ideal, the smooth ashlar acts as a lighthouse in the stormy seas of life. As we sail these waters, the waves of the world will buffet us one way or another and cause us to move in many a random course. However, by keeping sight of the ideal of the perfect ashlar, the Freemason is able to spot when they are moving off-course and correct their steering.

As an ideal for the whole of society, the high moral behaviour represented by the perfect ashlar is something important to aim for. However, the ideal of the utopian society, where everyone

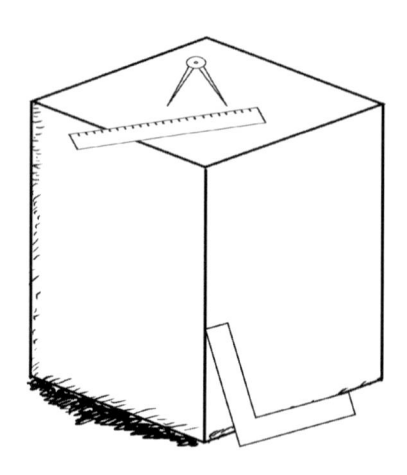

'The Pathway to the Perfect Ashlar Requires Continual Improvement'

is happy and where peace reigns forever, is unlikely to be fully realised. There will always be challenges and disappointments for human beings to face and to strive to overcome.

In many ways, we should be glad that life continually throws challenges at us. It is only when we are challenged that we catch glimpses of what we are capable of. Without the discomforts in life, we would become apathetic, and we would not grow. It has been recorded in history that creatures that are unable to change when circumstances change become extinct as a result of their inability to evolve. In this sense, it is a very important compulsion to be able to strive for continual change.

It is easy to see, then, that this too is something that has been passed down to us as the genetic heritage of our ancestors. It was because they had a continuous desire to change and to seek new resources to ensure survival that we now have the compulsion, deep down, to change ourselves. The greatest gift nature has given us is the ability to foresee issues that are not immediately apparent, and to cut these issues off before they happen.

It is perfectly natural, then, for human beings to look to the future and to imagine a better way to live. Moreover, this is evidenced in even the most mundane of our experiences, from the improvement of our domestic circumstances to our need to express ourselves more thoroughly at work.

It is for this reason that Freemasonry exists. It exists because we naturally want to grow. Therefore, it has developed a system by which consistent growth for the better can be experienced for the benefit of both the individual and the rest of society. It has carefully developed a system of psychological techniques and tools to help the Freemason in their endeavour, and an ideal to guide them on their way.

CHAPTER 7

KING SOLOMON'S TEMPLE AND SOCIETY

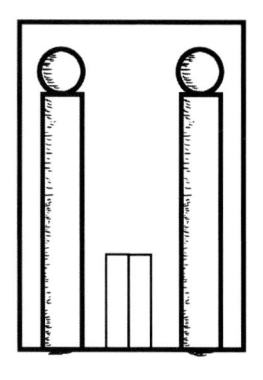

'The Entrance to King Solomon's Temple'

The journey of the Freemason, from the state symbolised by the rough ashlar, via the understanding of the application of the symbolic working-tools, to the state symbolised by the perfect ashlar, is intended to symbolically end in the placing of the stone into a symbolic building. Technically, any building that is made out of stone blocks would do. However, Freemasonry has a particular building in mind to act as the perfect symbol for the wider purpose of Freemasonry. That building is King Solomon's Temple.

The reason that this particular building is used in Freemasonry is because it is the ideal symbol for its purposes. It is the most important building mentioned in the Bible, which is just one expression of the Volume of the Sacred Law. When Freemasonry was developed in Europe, Christianity was the dominant religion, and it would have been this particular religion that the mediaeval stonemason would have subscribed to. Therefore, the most important building mentioned in the central scripture of Christianity would have been the most appropriate symbol recognisable to the Mason of that time.

King Solomon's Temple was particularly important in the Bible because it was considered to be the actual house of God. In modern times, we might use the term 'house of God' with reference to any church, but in the times of ancient Judaism it was taken to be literal in the case of the first temple. They believed that God actually lived there.

The entire structure was constructed to house the Ark of the Covenant, a golden casket that carried the original stone tablets on which the Ten Commandments were inscribed. This Ark was considered very holy and represented the covenant that God had with his people. The Jewish people at that time considered the Ark to be so holy that they carried it on golden staves wherever they went, covered up so that no one could lay eyes on it. It was so holy that human eyes could not even look upon it. Legend has it that people who tried to touch the Ark were stricken down dead. The Ark was the connection between God and His people, and signified to the Jews God's presence on the Earth.

Whilst out in the wilderness, when the people of Israel were stationary, a large tent was erected to house the Ark: this was consecrated and considered the holiest of places, no matter where it was. When the first temple of Jerusalem was constructed, it was created for one purpose alone, which was to act as a permanent resting-place for the Ark of the Covenant.

Once built, the temple had a special chamber inside it called the Holy of Holies. In other words, it was the one place in the world that was considered the most holy of all places. Once the Ark was initially placed in there no one could enter, apart from a priest at a particular time of year, and only then after that priest had ensured that he was entirely clean and pure.

Being a permanent place to house the Ark, and therefore the place where God was on the Earth, King Solomon's Temple was itself considered the holiest building in the whole world. Everything about it had to be perfect, as it was to be a house for God to call His home on Earth.

Walking into the Temple would have been a beautiful sight. Starting with the description of the Holy of Holies which, of course, nobody saw after the Ark was placed within it, this chamber was, as described in the Bible, twenty cubits in height, length and breadth, and the walls and floor were coated with gold. Also, inside the Holy of Holies were two giant cherubim, each ten cubits in height, between which the Ark was to be placed. The door to the Holy of Holies was also covered in gold, and was further covered by a veil coloured blue, red, and purple. These colours are particularly significant, because blue was seen to represent heaven, and red the realm of the flesh or the Earth, while purple is of course a mixture of these two colours: this colour scheme represented what the Holy of Holies actually was, namely the place where heaven and Earth met.

To ensure that no one could see into the Holy of Holies the door was closed and the veil drawn across the entrance. For the same reason, the chamber itself also had no windows.

Moving out of the Holy of Holies, we would come to some steps, and on descending the steps, we would find ourselves in a larger room that was known as the Greater House. The walls of this area were lined with cedar-wood on which were carved open flowers, pome-granates and cherubim. These walls and floor were also covered in gold.

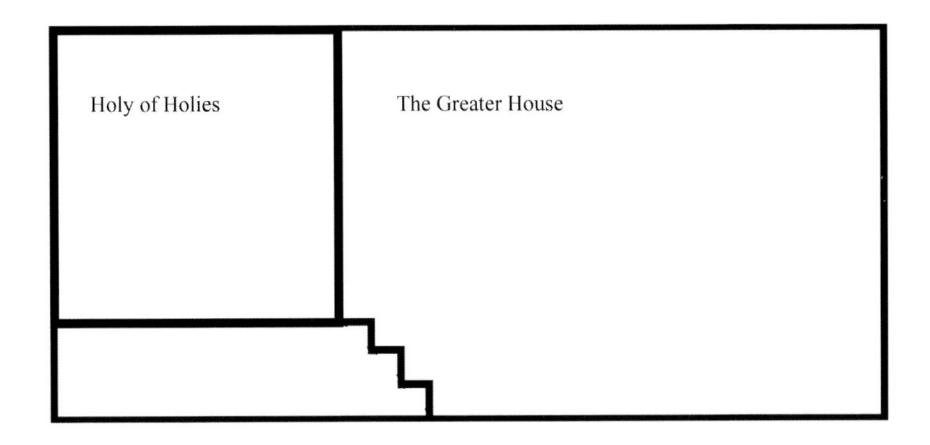

'Side Plan of King Solomon's Temple'

Similarly the doorway leading to this part of the Temple from the outside was made of olive-wood, had similar carvings on them to the walls and, like everything else, was covered in gold.

It is clear that King Solomon spared no expense in creating this grand building. Its very purpose was considered sufficient justification to use such precious materials. The best materials and workmen were employed for the job of building the temple and were supplied by Hiram, the King of Tyre.

This temple was essentially the centre of Jerusalem, and because of this, the city itself was considered the most holy of cities. Being a Jew in those times and being literally so close to where God is believed to have dwelt, must have been a very humbling experience. Going to pray at the temple was literally believed to be the same as going to God's house and asking Him personally.

It can be seen, then, that this temple is the ideal symbol for a Freemason. Since so much expense and effort went into the construction of this building it serves as a perfect benchmark for the stonemason to adhere to when crafting the materials of the building that they might be working on. However, for the speculative Freemason, the Temple itself represents much more.

It should be remembered that all Masonic lodges represent King Solomon's Temple, which is why lodge rooms are sometimes called temples. Therefore, all Freemasons meet inside a representation of the first temple at Jerusalem, and anything that the lodge room itself symbolises applies to the symbol of the temple itself.

Two things are symbolised by the Masonic lodge room: the macrocosm and the microcosm. The macrocosm is the wider Universe and everything in it, while the microcosm is considered to be the human being. In ancient times, in esoteric traditions, it was believed that the wider universe was related to the inner world of the human being. This is where the idea of the zodiac comes from, and why it was believed that the patterns of the stars and the movements of the planets could determine a human being's fate. Understanding the human mind was a way of understanding the wider universe, since in these traditions the two were related.

Therefore, the Freemason's lodge represents the universe at large. Ideally, the ceiling is painted in a dark blue colour, representing the night sky, and the zigzag pattern around the edge of the chequered floor of the lodge is supposed to represent the motion of the planets.

The black and white floor itself represents the opposites encountered in life, like light and dark, good and evil, difficult and easy, or beautiful and ugly. The Masonic Candidate moves around the lodge on this Masonic flooring, showing the pathway of a Mason through their life and through the trials and tribulations we all encounter in our lives.

The two Wardens in the lodge represent the sun and the moon, and the orientation of the lodge room is according to the compass points. The entrance to the lodge is in the West, where the sun sets, the East being at the other end, where the Master sits, representing the rising sun.

If we compare the Masonic lodge room, based as it is on the wider universe, with the original temple at Jerusalem, we can see how the latter might represent the universe at large, with God situated at its centre. Remember that flowers, pomegranates and various foliage were inscribed on the walls of the temple, which represents the natural world.

The microcosm, as has already been mentioned, is also represented by the Masonic lodge room, and it is here where we can further relate the lodge to the idea of initiation. With the aid of the officers within a Masonic lodge we can see how initiation works and how initiation can be seen to be a journey within oneself.

Outside the door of the lodge stands the Tyler, who is essentially a guard to prevent any unqualified person from entering the meeting taking place inside. Psychologically speaking, this person represents the ability to be selective in what we see and hear. It is all too easy to believe everything that we hear, and we must be discerning so that we can get a more accurate representation of the world in our minds. For instance, it is well known that we should be mindful of listening to gossip, since we could end up getting the wrong idea about a person when that idea could be unjustified. Essentially, anything that we allow into our minds should be as accurate as possible, and tested with our sense of logic and insight. If we don't know anything about a person, or a situation, we should be mindful of exactly what we observe and seek to learn more about them from experience.

Inside the door of the lodge, there stands the Inner Guard, who acts as a double-measure of security for the lodge. This insistence on ensuring that no one unqualified enters the lodge room backs up the psychological need to be aware of what we allow into our minds. However, the Inner Guard also has the job of allowing people out of the room if they leave. This represents the psychological faculty of being mindful of what one says. Everyone knows that some of what we say can be inappropriate and hurtful, so we should be mindful of every situation in which we might need to choose our words carefully. Another instance of being careful of what we say is when people confide in us. The trust that has been placed in us when we are asked to keep a secret is fundamental to the stability of that particular relationship. Any information that a person doesn't want disclosing should be kept firmly within one's mind.

Of course, it is also important to be aware of how we speak to people, and therefore clear and articulate speech should always be our preferred style of communication.

Once past the door of the lodge there are other officers that have special significance psychologically. The first of these officers are the Deacons, whose job it is to lead the Candidate around the lodge room during an initiation ceremony. The Deacon's job is to ensure that the Candidate knows what to say at particular parts of the ceremony. Psychologically, this represents the part of us that seems to aid us in our endeavours through life. Whenever we start something new, it is likely that we are not fully aware of what is to be expected of us. The unknown in any new situation can instil fear in us, since the psychological make-up of a human being keeps us safe by guiding us away from unknown situations where there might be danger. However, by understanding that we are capable of more than we initially think we are we can boldly step into undiscovered territory, no matter what or where it might be in life. The voice of the Deacon prompting the Candidate in their ear is the same as this guiding principle that helps us in new situations. The Deacons carry long wands that have dove symbols on the top indicating that they are messengers. In the Christian tradition, the dove also symbolises the Holy Spirit. The Freemason, therefore, should always remember that they have a guiding principle within that will help them.

We should all remember that nowadays human beings are far more capable than they were in prehistoric times. Our species has been around for hundreds of thousands of years, and we have had that time to evolve a survival instinct that can cope with new situations. Over the time that mankind has existed, the main threat to us has been changes in the environment, yet, no matter how uncomfortable the state of the world has got we have always found ways of coping.

In fact, when tough situations arise this is exactly when most creatures evolve and advance themselves. It seems to be the tough and difficult situations that are the very crucible of development.

As modern-day human beings, we have all inherited a survival capability from our highly successful ancestors. Therefore, if we only listen to the voice within, we can solve any new problem that comes our way. We should always welcome the potentially transformative challenges we might face and so we should never be afraid to walk into the unknown to advance ourselves.

After the two Deacons in the lodge, there are the two Wardens: the Junior Warden, and the Senior Warden. The Junior Warden represents both beauty and the sun.

Beauty is a quality that most of us recognise, and it seems to be fundamental to the workings of our mind. When human beings design anything, there appears to be a need to provide it with a certain aesthetic quality. Usually, these aesthetic qualities differ over time but, in every age, human beings seem to have a fundamental understanding of what is beautiful and what is not. One theory suggests that our sense of beauty is related to what is known as the Golden Mean. This Golden Mean is the value of 1.618, and it is known that many things in nature are constructed according to a ratio based on this number. For instance, if one measures the length of the last bone that forms the tip of the index finger and divides that value by the length of the next bone along, the result is the Golden Mean. This is true when dividing the finger-bone joining to the rest of the hand by the length of the middle bone as well. Dividing the total height of a typical human by the distance between the floor and the navel will also result in a number around the value of the Golden Mean.

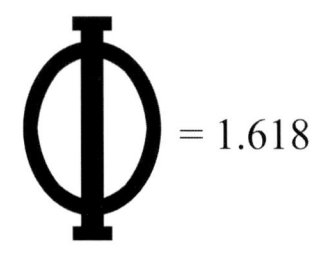

$\Phi = 1.618$

'The Golden Mean'

Not only is the Golden Mean found in humans but also in other natural phenomena such as dividing the relative distances of the arms of a spiral galaxy, and in the spiral arms of a snail-shell.

We tend to find faces that are more closely built around the relative distances that result in the Golden Mean more beautiful than those faces that do not, and this fact alone suggests that beauty must have something to do with the Golden Mean.

Whatever the source of the beauty that we experience in the world, we always automatically know when we have seen something beautiful. It appears to be an emotion that is the fruit of an experience that cannot easily be explained to other people. All we can do when someone says they find something beautiful is to relate it to the memory of the feeling we have when we experience beauty.

Beauty, then, would seem to stir within us something truly non-communicable and transcendent. To experience beauty, or any emotion, is to experience what some might call the soul, or spirit. Whatever one calls it, it helps remind us of the non-tangible quality of ourselves, and thus that which connects us with the ground of all being. This is why people find walks in the countryside so fulfilling. The innate beauty experienced in the natural world has the power to connect us to ourselves.

The other thing that the Junior Warden represents is the sun which, being the source of natural light, represents the source of knowledge. This symbol reminds the Freemason of the need to educate themselves, as pointed out by the symbolism of the chisel in the First Degree. To enlighten the mind with knowledge helps the Freemason to understand the world around them and to render themselves more serviceable to mankind. However, we must remember that this knowledge doesn't just mean trying to understand facts about the world and our place in it, but should also imply an understanding of the Self. In order to do this, we need to be able to experience as much of life as we possibly can. We need to ensure, as suggested by the symbolism of the Deacons, that we constantly challenge ourselves. If we are not constantly challenging ourselves then we can never be sure that we are not capable of more. Those who remain in their comfort-zones may think that they know who they are and what they are capable of, but stepping outside this comfort-zone would enable them to see if there is any more capability within to do and to learn and to be more.

Of course, the constant moving out of the comfort-zone in pursuit of self-knowledge might not suit everyone. A human being can be quite happy in many diverse situations, and there is nothing wrong with this. However, if a human being wishes to maximise their usefulness to society and discover the inner secrets of themselves then a good way of doing it is to provide oneself with challenges, no matter how big or small.

The Senior Warden in the lodge also represents two things, namely the quality of strength and the Moon.

Strength is required in all our endeavours; it is not simply a faculty that is associated with one's physical muscles, but is more a quality of mind. Many feats commonly associated with physical strength actually have their origin in a strong mind. Any time spent in a gym will quickly show that straining the muscles involves an element of discomfort, and yet, in order to benefit from the exercise, a person needs to keep moving through the discomfort. Keeping going despite feelings of discomfort screaming that one should cease the activity is entirely dependent on mental resource.

The same can be said for the long-distance runner. Even though the athlete might have trained their body to the optimum state for long distance, the muscles will still complain after a while. If the runner gave in to the signals from their muscles then they would stop and end up not finishing the race. This, again, is more an example of the strength of mind required for physical activity.

True strength is a state of mind, and also comes in useful in all situations that are not usually associated with physical strength. For instance, mental strength can carry us through various difficult situations that we must necessarily pass through in life. Yet, mental strength is also required to enable us to achieve any worthwhile endeavour. If a person wishes to become a millionaire then they must first find a way of providing a service that people will want to pay them money for. First attempts at this are rarely successful, and the entrepreneur must pass through many experiences of failure before a working solution is settled upon.

However, it is the failures that one experiences that help hone the solution that eventually succeeds, and mental strength of purpose is required to carry us through each failure and on to eventual success. One famous example of this strength of mind and character is Thomas Edison. When asked how he wasn't put off by the many failed solutions on his journey to inventing the light-bulb, said that he didn't fail many times, he merely found many ways in which a light-bulb wouldn't work, and so kept going until he found a way where it could work.

Strength of mind is an essential quality if we are to make a success of our life; it is the one thing that enables us to have integrity. Each of us has a unique personality that has developed because of our particular experiences in life. Each of us is unique and so has something of value to offer the world. Sometimes, we encounter the types of people who might wish to impose their will over us, and not wish to take into consideration the fact that we might be useful in any given situation. It is therefore imperative that we have enough strength of character so that we may stand as individuals and make ourselves heard, as we deserve.

Of course, having enough resolve to stand as strong characters requires confidence and a self-belief that we can indeed be useful. This can only come through experience and insight into ourselves: to understand that we have a unique perspective on the world and that this unique perspective should be added to the mix of perspectives and can help to move everything forward.

The Senior Warden also represents the moon: this is the principle in man that is illuminated by the divine light represented by the sun rising in the East. In very ancient times, the sun was associated with divinity. It was the light of the sun that brought life and purpose to everything and was literally the origin of the life principle. Furthermore, it is the light of the sun that illuminates the moon. Without it, the moon would be invisible at night. Therefore the moon represents the faculty that casts the light of knowledge to penetrate the darkness of ignorance.

As the Freemason progresses through their journey, they are slowly chipping away at their inner worlds

'The Ionic Column, Representing Wisdom'

so that they might arrive at the fundamental principle within. As has been mentioned throughout this book, the purpose of initiation is to unite the individual with the transcendent whole in order to discover the truths that are hidden beneath the surface of experience. Once this principle has been discovered, it then has the effect of enlightening the mind of the Initiate. Like the moon, the mind has been illuminated by the light that is continually emitted from the source, animating and sustaining all things, so that their behaviour is forever changed in favour of spreading the benefit of this illumination within their daily lives through their moral standpoint and their day-to-day interactions with other people.

Finally, the officer in charge of the whole lodge is the Master of the lodge, who represents both wisdom and the light that shines from the East.

Wisdom is an interesting subject. It is often confused with knowledge, but this does not quite offer a complete definition of what wisdom actually is. Certainly, wisdom requires knowledge. However, that knowledge only enables us to engage more with the world around us and encourages the faculty of wisdom to flourish. Wisdom also requires experience, because acquiring facts is one thing, while spending time applying and experiencing the things that comprise this knowledge is entirely another. A good example of this is a person's ability to spot patterns over time. A younger person might be quite vulnerable to distress and negative feelings if life doesn't always go their way. After enough of their life has elapsed and that person has got older though, they may find themselves less adversely affected by the downturns of life, after having experienced many times over that downturns usually end and that life returns to normal, or even has high points.

Wisdom is a quality that seems to enable us to better navigate life, and can sometimes be experienced as though it has come from somewhere within us, as if there is a well or spring which can sometimes be tapped. A person can even surprise themselves when, in situations like the giving of advice to other people, they seem to land on a solution that the other person could use which seemed to have just appeared in their minds, and which they hadn't ever thought of before. It is as if the words have just flowed from some deeper place, because they haven't required any obvious conscious pondering to produce them.

These kinds of experiences show that the human mind is more capable than we give it conscious credit for. For years, psychologists have known that there are two main aspects of human consciousness: the conscious mind and the subconscious mind. The conscious mind is where all of our experiences rest. It acts like a torch in the darkness, illuminating wherever it is pointed. Whatever we are aware of at any given moment actually falls within a very small area of total consciousness, while the darkness represents everything else in our minds, or the subconscious. The subconscious mind represents the rest of our brain that is not currently supplying the contents of direct consciousness. This means the majority of the awesome power of the brain acts unconsciously. This part of the mind is still thinking, but you are unaware of it. When we surprise ourselves with some piece of wisdom that appears to have come from nowhere, it is because this faculty has passed a potential solution to the attention of the conscious mind.

It must be remembered that the brain filters out what we could potentially be aware of through our senses, leaving only the information that is relevant to our current survival for our conscious minds to deal with. However, all of the data that our sense organs can directly perceive is pumped straight into the brain. The conscious mind gets the abridged version of what is going on around and within those sense organs, but the rest is there in the brain, being processed as silent thoughts. This is why the source of wisdom seems to be so accurate, because it results from using data that represents a more complete picture of the world.

In many ways, this function that the brain has of taking everything in connects it directly with the ongoing evolution of the universe, helping us to find our ideal place in the world if we could but find a way to tap into it. The subconscious is constantly picking up clues from the world around us, and these clues are often communicated through feelings or urges that we ought to act on in a particular situation. We might, for instance, feel the urge to take up painting in order to express something that we think about often and deeply. Perhaps then it is important to, with discretion, follow these emotions, as they might well be the result of subconscious thoughts which have arisen from the processing of data gathered from the wider world around us. Perhaps there is a such a thing as destiny after all.

The light from the East that the Master also represents is directly related to the faculty of wisdom. As has been mentioned, the sun rises in the East to enlighten the day, just as the fundamental principle behind all things can be discovered within the Self. The source of wisdom that shines within comes, as we have seen, from the subconscious mind processing the wider world. This wider world, in turn, rests on processes that are based on the fundamental principle or principles that sustain the existence of the universe, and which were there at its inception. Even though this fundamental principle transcends human understanding, it can certainly illuminate the mind from within as we get into closer contact with our subconscious minds or our deeper selves, and this is helped by the concept of initiation and self-reflection over time. Truly we can come into contact with the transcendent in this way.

Throughout the Freemason's career, they will advance through the offices from Inner Guard to the Master of the lodge. This, in itself, is part of the journey of Freemasonry. The taking up of each office, in turn, symbolises the embodiment of each of the different aspects of the inner human psyche. As the Freemason contemplates the faculty represented by the office they hold, they slowly come to an understanding of their total inner life and, as they progress towards the chair of the Master of the lodge, they are following a symbolic pathway deeper and deeper into the Self, culminating in the source of wisdom represented by the Master. This symbolic journey should mirror the development of the individual's conscious mind as they establish more and more of a connection with their innermost selves.

Returning to the idea that the Masonic lodge is representative of King Solomon's Temple, we can see how the first temple at Jerusalem can be seen to represent the microcosm, or the inner world of the human being. Entering the Temple would be like entering through the door of the lodge, and the symbolic journey through the offices is like the approach towards the Holy of Holies in which lies the presence of the source of all things. Remember, the interior of the Holy of Holies was shrouded from the view of everyone, just as the processes of the subconscious are shrouded from the inspection of the conscious mind. However, as we approach the door to this sacred chamber we come closer to that transcendent source of wisdom that is one with the workings of the whole universe.

To further illustrate the connection between King Solomon's temple and the inner psyche, we should remember the winding staircase of the Second Degree. This staircase ascended from the ground, twisting and turning its way to the doors of the middle chamber of the temple. The stairs are going up, indicating that the journey of the Freemason's consciousness is slowly being elevated, and they arrive at the door to the middle chamber of the temple, where the Masons get their reward, showing that the upward-moving journey is also an inward-moving Journey.

Having learned how King Solomon's temple can represent both the wider universe and the inner human being, and demonstrated how these two are connected, it probably won't be too surprising to learn that there is another thing the ancient temple at Jerusalem is meant to represent: human society as a whole.

The job of Freemasonry, as has been mentioned many times, is to lead the Initiate on a journey within themselves, so that they might be better enabled to understand the world and how it interconnects with them. This inner self-discovery is for the particular purpose, however, of using the understanding acquired through initiation for the benefit of the rest of mankind.

King Solomon's Temple was chosen as a symbol because it was the most perfect building in the Bible, as it was designed to house the spirit of God. Therefore, the aim of Freemasonry is to help guide humanity to become the best it can be. By using the symbol of crafting a stone block to represent the crafting of the individual human being, the message is that the general improvement of society will ultimately come from the hard work of individuals who understand that a society is a collection of people. And that if that society is to improve the people must be prepared to improve themselves.

Just as the block that has been crafted for a specific purpose is placed into the wider structure so that it can do its job in supporting the building, the Masonic Initiate crafts himself for the specific purpose of helping to support society. Yet this support can only be achieved in relationship with other people, just as the job of a piece of masonry is only achieved through the pieces that surround it. Therefore, human beings need to be able to work hand in hand with other individuals in the world, which requires respect and understanding.

Human beings have a long history of not getting along. There always seems to be a war, or battle, or some sort of a dispute somewhere in the world. Yet we need to move beyond our differences. We must all understand that we are all partakers in life and that we are all subject to similar problems. Mankind could really flourish if it simply chose to stop fighting and, instead, work together to a brighter future, to the benefit of everybody.

When we understand that each person around has something valid to offer the world then we are better enabled to work with them in order to create a more stable society. After all, society requires everyone to take responsibility for the general state of how mankind is organised, just as, in a building, no element of the structure is wasted and everything takes its share of the load. Society simply cannot operate optimally if there are elements who do not pull their weight. Just as a building will stand easily when everything is together, but each time you take out a stone block an extra load is placed on the blocks that are still in-situ. As one keeps taking more blocks away, the extra load gets shared out everywhere else, until the remaining elements cannot perform the extra task as well as their own, and the building collapses.

Therefore, in order for society to stand strong and healthy, it cannot have too many elements that are not providing support. Obvious examples of this come from the economy where people go to work in order to earn money to feed, clothe, and house themselves and their families, as well as to enable them to create and experience things they want to experience in life. In some countries, there is also a support mechanism to assist those who cannot work to earn money. However, in those places with support mechanisms, there is also an element of the population that are quite able to work but instead take advantage of the system, so they can get money without having to expend any effort in return. Some are very good at this and manage to extort many thousands from the public coffers, enabling them to enjoy some experiences that even those who work struggle to afford.

These rogue elements of economic society may be acting under the idea that they shouldn't have to waste their life working when they could be enjoying what life has to offer. This, on the face of it, seems like a very sound and fair idea, but the holes in the scheme soon become apparent. In order for society to exist in a healthy state, everyone needs to be able to eat, be clothed, be sheltered, and feel safe. These things are pretty much the bare minimum for survival. However, the food needs to be produced, delivered and sold. Clothing needs to be designed, produced, delivered, and sold. Houses need to be built. Where machines are used to help production, people are required to design and build those machines. Education is required to teach people how to do these jobs. The list goes on, but this does show that even the simplest things we take for granted require people to go to work and produce them. In return for going to work, they get paid money which, in turn, gets ploughed back into the economy for the buying of goods and services. Moreover, with the variety of goods and services available for people in the world to enjoy, and innovation happening all the time, it seems obvious that there is room for everyone to be able to work and provide some useful service to society.

Where the burden is most felt is when it comes to taxation. Almost everyone who goes to work pays taxes, depending on the tax rules of the country in which they live. These taxes go into paying for public services and the running of the country as a whole. Some of the revenue from these taxes also goes towards the support system that is intended to help those who are unable to work to earn their own money. Clearly, when people take advantage of the support system, but do not really need the help, they are putting an unnecessary burden on society as a whole. Ultimately, taxes need to rise to pay the extra money paid out to the people who take advantage and, eventually, the working people start to feel the pinch and society in its entirety begins ever so slightly to crumble.

The debt economy is yet another example of how society can be unbalanced and can begin to unravel. The problem here comes directly from modern-day consumerist culture. Every day, people are shown ways of life that they ought to aspire to; lives replete with nice cars, exotic holidays, large houses, and fancy restaurants. Yet, these lifestyles are incredibly expensive to maintain and are most likely beyond most people's income. To help things along, however, organisations like banks and credit-card companies offer the service of extra credit, so long as we pay that credit back, with interest.

Obviously, people access these extra credit services in order to access the good life that is promised by the media. The more credit that is accessed the more a person owes, and so they end up being trapped in debt, using most of their income paying off loans which they possibly don't even have anything to show for anymore. Since income is spent paying back credit, there is less to buy necessities and to help lead a stress-free life, so more credit is required. This is what is called a debt cycle which, itself, starts to dry up once a person has borrowed as much as their credit rating will allow. Thus, if enough people do this, society ends up in a situation where people default on their payments, the money which was loaned is never paid back, people get into trouble, stop buying goods and services, people lose their jobs due to a fall in custom, and then everything begins to fall around our ears as a society.

This is an example of where banks and similar financial institutions do not serve society. By extending loans and credit to people who want it, they actually end up putting extra load on various other interconnected parts of the larger community. It is an example of unsound business activity, of selfish activity, which ends up causing issues further afield and eventually ends up coming full circle and affecting the financial institutions that acted unsoundly in the first place.

Clearly, then, everyone – both individuals and institutions – need to understand that they are part of an intricate web of causation, much like a building is composed of elements, each of which bear a load and affect each other. Each time an individual or group of individuals act, for better or for worse, it has an effect on everyone else to greater or lesser extent.

This lesson should also be understood with regard to the environment in which we all live. How we treat our planet will ultimately have an effect on all of us. Despite the fact that some of us recycle, there still isn't enough being done. Everything we don't recycle goes into a landfill site which will affect the surrounding environment. We pollute our seas with rubbish and chemicals, affecting the creatures that live there.

In the past, we have over-hunted animals, and to this day, we tend to hunt animals to near-extinction. This has a wide-ranging effect. Imagine that a species of wolf is hunted to extinction in a particular area. As a result of the absence of this natural predator, the herbivorous animals on which they used to prey begin to grow in population. The growth in the population of these animals cause more of the vegetation to be stripped bare, and the bushes and trees which used to grow in the area no longer flourish. Since there aren't enough trees, the bird population that used to nest in the trees is reduced to zero. As a result of the absence of birds, the insects that they used to feed on are no longer kept in check.

From taking one animal out of the picture, the entire ecosystem is altered because of the intricate connections between all things. Animals find a natural equilibrium with their environment, but we move beyond what could be called our natural balance and have tended to utilise the resources of the world as we wish, without any thought of how our actions change everything, which, eventually, will have an impact on human civilisation.

Thankfully, this is changing, and we are becoming far more aware of how we affect the world. Yet, more work needs to be done before we can safely say that we live in balance with the world at large.

The symbol of King Solomon's Temple can be applied here if we see it as representing society and, indeed, the wider world. Again, it shows the interdependency of the relative parts of the world on many levels.

King Solomon's Temple was built for the specific purpose of housing the Ark of the Covenant, which was considered to be where the divine met with the Earth. With this in mind, and seeing the Temple as a symbol for the interrelationships necessary for the ideal functioning of society, we can conclude that Freemasonry sees a correctly functioning society as centred around a divine principle.

In modern times, many would disagree that such a spiritual foundation is required for a forward-thinking civilisation, and that the only thing that religion tends to do is divide society. In some sense, it is true that the many different religions of the world do cause many tribal splits. However, it has been argued throughout this book that there does indeed exist a fundamental principle to the universe that transcends human understanding. Not only does it underlie everything in the material universe, it also provides the foundation for our experience. Therefore, it is possible to connect with our deeper selves to come closer to this overall transcendent creative source. Within religions, this principle is called deity, and the different religions attempt to express how one should live in order to approach this divine reality.

It is important to remember, though, that the religions of the world are constructed in different geographic areas and are written in the context of widely different cultural histories and traditions. All of the scriptures of any culture were written by human hands, even if it was claimed that what has been written is through divine inspiration. We must consider that what is written is as a result of a human mind, which will naturally interpret what it has observed in its own unique way, depending on the person's background, and that this person will express it using their particular command of verbal expression. Therefore, different religions might be massively different, but they do all point to a fundamental principle. If all the religions of the world can be seen as an expression of the singular transcendent reality that exists behind all things, we no longer have any need to claim that one religion is superior to another. What we have is a set of different religions, each with their own take on a singular transcendent principle. People would feel free to study the content of a faith that was not their own, and people would begin to converge on the truth.

The image of society being built around a central transcendent principle then can still work. Even with diverse belief systems in the world, the simple acceptance of each religion as a genuine perspective will allow mutual respect.

People who claim to be atheists can still see value in this model of society, because it is obvious that the origin of all things can be approached through scientific examination alongside the emotional, inner psychological exploration that can be embarked upon when appreciating a beautiful work of art that challenges perceptual concepts. It is not necessary to see the source of all things as a God, since God is simply a word that conveys a dim shadow of the true reality. There is indeed something that originated the universe, which, ultimately, can only truly be understood in part.

The main feature that King Solomon's Temple highlights is the need for interdependent relationships for society to function properly. Human civilisation cannot work properly if people act from the position of the Self, and don't acknowledge the greater need for selflessly directed action.

In the next chapter, we will see that acting selfishly is potentially based on an erroneous philosophy. We need to explore the possibility, as expressed in some philosophies that the Self that we all think exists, doesn't exist at all.

CHAPTER 8

THE ILLUSION OF THE SELF AND THE TRUTH OF INTERDEPENDENCY

'Om, the Divine Symbol of Hinduism'

The journey of the Freemason cannot be completed, in actuality, by simply experiencing the three parts of initiation represented by the Three Degrees. The initiation ceremonies themselves are only intended to be springboards for further contemplation. The initiation process must involve, by necessity, a certain degree of experimentation in the laboratory of one's own life. The true meaning and usefulness of the symbols presented in the Degrees of Freemasonry can only ever be understood by attempting to utilise what they represent in everyday living.

Therefore, the majority of the journey of the Freemason takes place outside the doors of the lodge, in the wider world. As the Freemason goes through life using the working-tools, they gradually uncover aspects of themselves and understand their connection with those around them. This entire process involves a great deal of looking inward and introspection, and it would seem at first glance that Freemasonry is too focused on the Self.

Freemasonry, in general, has an outward-looking focus. Freemasonry promotes charitable giving and encourages its members to render themselves more serviceable to the wider community, so being a Freemason is meant to be about living selflessly. In order to help a Masonic Initiate to embrace selfless action, Masonic initiation is designed to help the Candidate to further understand the nature of the Self and how it relates to the rest of the world.

However, the concept of the Self is not always as clear-cut as it might at first seem. Ordinarily, we use the term 'Self' to refer to the watcher that appears to experience the world from inside our bodies. There is a sense that we somehow live somewhere behind our faces, looking out through the windows that we call the eyes. The term 'Self' mainly refers to feelings and conscious experience directly, but we do not always use the same term to refer to our physicality. To explain further, we would generally refer to ourselves in conversation by using the words 'I' or 'me.' These are both words that relate directly to the concept of the Self, but we also use terms like 'my body' to refer to our flesh-and-blood presence. It would appear that we have a sense that we exist as an entity within our bodies and that this entity owns that body but is not entirely defined by it.

What, then, is actually defining itself by using words like 'I'? The most obvious candidate would appear to be the brain. After all, everything we think, say, or do can be matched up to activity in our central nervous systems. However, we also refer to this lump of grey matter as 'my brain.' This would imply there is something that perhaps exists separately from the brain, which is in possession of, but not entirely defined by, a brain.

Clearly, it is this feeling that gives rise to the sense that we exist as an entity that is integral yet separate from our bodies. There indeed seems to exist, a Self. Yet, if this Self exists then where and what is it?

Many traditions have sought to answer this question. One religious argument is that there is a soul, or essential spirit, that represents the true nature of the Self, and that our bodies are merely vessels for this essential Self. This particular idea gives rise to the concept that the soul continues after death, and that our ultimate destinies lie elsewhere, beyond this life.

In India, the ancient tradition of Hinduism developed the idea that there was a world soul, called Brahman, and a personal soul, called Atman. Essentially, the personal soul was simply one expression of the world soul, as if the world soul was dreaming that it was each thing simultaneously. Early Indian traditions were examples of some of the earliest ideas about the connection between the individual and the ground of all being. As has been covered in earlier chapters, the process of initiation such as that found in Freemasonry is designed so that the mind of the Initiate might discover some sense of union with the transcendent foundation within them.

However, these conceptions of the nature of the Self appear to arise from how we experience the sense of Self. At first appearance, we do indeed seem to inhabit our bodies rather than actually be those bodies.

Rather than accepting the concept of the Self as an entity in its own right, the tradition of Buddhism seeks to analyse the phenomenon of experience in order to yield more rationally satisfying answers with regard to its origin. Buddhism suggests that if we really look for the origin of that which we take as a separately existing Self we will ultimately find that it is merely an illusion. From the Buddhist perspective, everything in the universe exists as a result of Dependent Arising. This means that, according to this philosophy, the world we seem to take as containing objects that exist as entities in their own right does not exist as we think it does.

When asked to imagine a table, the image that comes to our mind's eye is a flat surface usually supported by four legs, and maybe constructed out of wood. The philosophy of Dependent Arising implies that what we think is a table is not a table at all but is, in actual fact, a collection of pieces of wood, namely the flat surface and the four pieces of wood that act as legs. If we look more closely at one of these legs then the idea of Dependent Arising again suggests that this piece of wood is not a piece of wood as it might first seem but is, in fact, a collection of certain kinds of carbon-based molecules. In other words, everything that we take for granted as existing in and of itself, actually depends on smaller elements for its existence.

In fact, the philosophy of Dependent Arising implies that the world we see exists because the mind defines and labels it. The world cannot exist without the involvement of the mind.

A table exists because the mind sees its construction and calls it a table. The human mind cannot perceive the essential constituents of matter like molecules and atoms: it can only perceive grosser objects, and accepts them as solid objects which, being constructed from atoms, they clearly aren't. Buddhism holds that if anything *were* to exist in and of itself then it wouldn't be possible to analyse it any further into its constituent parts.

If everything exists as a result of Dependent Arising, that would mean the concept of the Self must also exist because of Dependent Arising. To illustrate this further, we merely need to imagine a human being instead of a table. Looking at this imaginary human being, we would at first imagine that this person's Self must be represented by the totality of the person's physical presence. How much then would this person have to lose before he stopped being a Self? Imagine we took their arms away, they would still be considered the same Self, yet with no arms. The same would occur if we took the legs away: the detached arms and legs would be considered as mere pieces that had come away and would not correspond to the Self we are looking for in the person. The Self, we seem to automatically take for granted, is somewhere in the body and head that is left behind.

Now, we are left with two pieces of this person's body, and, it is here that something slightly curious happens. If we take off the only limb-like structure left, the head, it is not the body that we assume houses the Self, but the head. The body, having come away from the head, has simply become another piece that has fallen away. It would seem, to no great surprise that we see the Self as being in the head. Yet we can go still further, reducing this head to just the brain and, again, we would have discarded everything else as simply bits and pieces, all apart from the brain that we are certain contains the Self.

The next obvious thing is to take away parts of the brain. As we do this, piece by piece, we always tend to see what we have left as being the seat of the Self, and not the parts of the brain that we are taking away. Yet, whilst all this is happening, the person we are dissecting, so long as his brain remains conscious, is aware of certain faculties disappearing, but nevertheless continues to experience himself as a Self, right up the moment when he loses consciousness. What we find is that the concept of the Self is dependent on the interconnections of the brain and is not, in fact, something that exists in and of itself. Are we saying that the Self is the brain? No. What we are saying is that the brain, as a complex structure, appears to generate our sense of Self.

What our sense of Self actually is can be very difficult to define, and indeed it may never be correctly defined. The nature of experience is a deep mystery that appears to transcend scientific scrutiny. However, what we do seem to be fairly confident about is that our sense of Self feels as if it is inside us, mainly inside our heads. This doesn't come as too

THE ILLUSION OF THE SELF AND THE TRUTH OF INTERDEPENDENCY | 143

much of a surprise, given that most of our sense organs are situated in our head. If we remember that our brains are learning machines then we can construct a model of how the location of this sense of Self is generated.

First, take the ears. They feed auditory data into the brain from both sides of the skull. The mechanisms associated with the ear enable the brain to determine from which side a source of sound is coming from more strongly, and this is how the brain can work out where, in space, the source of the sound is.

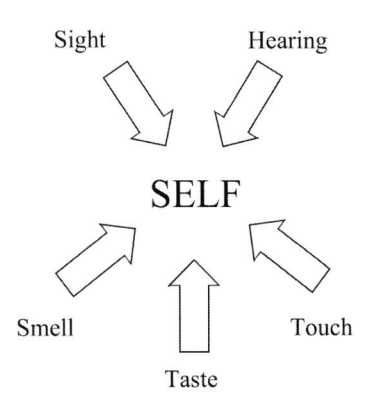

'Calculating the Sense of Self'

However, the brain is also easily tricked into concluding that it exists as separate from the sense of sound. Although it may appear to the brain that the experience of sound is a separate entity to itself, it is, in fact, a representation generated by the brain.

If we add sight to this analysis, then we have a similar situation that further compounds the problem of the generation of the sense of a Self that is separate from the world of sense. The brain is able to come to the conclusion that it can be located somewhere between hearing data and sight data.

Bring in the remaining three senses of taste, touch, and smell, and the definition of the Self is made more concrete. The Self becomes that thing that may be found situated between sight, hearing, touch, smell and taste. This is how our sense of Self is calculated by our brains. It is, perhaps, almost as if the brain is able to geolocate itself in the world with respect to the senses.

By using the senses, the brain locates itself in the world and calls this the Self. This process is not simply limited to sense data, however. The thoughts that pass through our minds are also a type of data-stream, experienced in the same way as the five senses. In other words, the brain sees itself located somewhere between each of the five senses and thoughts. Thoughts are seen as separate from the brain in the same way that senses are. This gives rise to the common terms such as 'my senses' or 'my thoughts', which tell us that from one point of view these elements are clearly owned by a Self.

However, we can now be fairly certain that impulses from each of our senses create the firing of groups of neurons in particular parts of the brain. These neuronal firings are the sense data being processed, leading to our sense of experience. Everything that arises from our senses seems to be inseparable from the grey matter of the brain. It is also clear that thought process consist of neuronal firings in the brain, again inseparable from the brain.

Despite the conclusion of the brain that there is a Self, separate from the world, it turns out that our only direct knowledge of the world comes from these senses that are processed within the brain. We never see the world directly, but only as an interpretation via the processes of our central nervous system. In reality, our sense of Self is one with our sense of the world, and it is also one with our sense of the thought processes. In fact, the very notion of our sense of Self turns out to be the result of a thought process, one which takes all the senses and thoughts which we experience and then calculates a location for the Self within the body. Our sense of Self is a thought.

In this sense, using the notion of Dependent Arising, the Self is not the brain and it does not reside within the brain. It is dependent on the thought processes made possible through the interconnections of the central nervous system. The Self does not exist in and of itself.

The idea that a Self does not exist has an effect on how we view the world. It gives rise to the notion that we do not directly experience the world, but instead are only experiencing what our brain's interpretation tells us, and that we can have no direct knowledge of anything in the world without a human mind being involved, usually our own. Our knowledge of the world is entirely dependent on how good our brains are at providing an accurate report, and the kind of report that our brains offer our conscious awareness is often dependent on the state of our brains at the time. We have perhaps all experienced a similar situation of buying a car and then suddenly seeing the same model of car everywhere on the road, whereas we could swear this wasn't the case previously. Clearly, the number of models of this car has not suddenly undergone an overnight increase in our area, but is because our brains are now keyed in to recognising that car, because we now own that model.

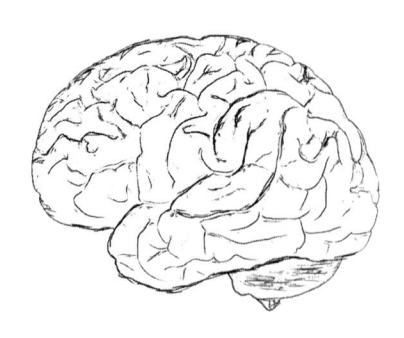

'The Brain Contains the Self as a Thought Process'

Similarly, we all know that the world can look different depending on our moods. If we are in a bad mood then we tend to see the world in a negative way. However, if we are in a good mood we experience the converse: a more positive world. Once again this works on the same principle that accounts for the mysterious increase in the same type of car you bought. The mind tends to find the things it is primed to observe, and so you will tend to observe things around you that will match and support your mood.

These very simple but widely known examples indicate, in an obvious way, how our minds affect what we experience of the world, and that no form of experience ever exists without our minds being involved. Therefore, not only can we never directly understand a world that is not coloured by the human mind, we cannot directly know another human being other than the representation which we have in our mind. This is why first impressions are so important: if our first meeting with someone is positive, we are more likely to conclude that the person we met is likeable, but if they are negative, we will conclude that the person is not likeable. However, the conclusions we have come to are not in any way related to how likeable the person actually is: they only reflect the interpretation we have given to a very limited set of sense data. Clearly, we should always maintain an open mind about people.

Successfully maintaining an open mind with regard to the people around us tends to improve our ability to forgive others. Knowing we do not always have the full information about why a person does things discourages us from judging anyone conclusively.

The impossibility of direct knowledge of other people also seems to apply to the knowledge of oneself. The only knowledge we have about ourselves is constructed out of memories of sensory data. We know how we appear to have acted at particular times. We know what we are likely to think and feel in particular situations. However, as has been indicated, all of this sensory data has been filtered through our brains. The ideas of ourselves that we have now are not necessarily complete pictures of who we really are. This offers us a lot of scope in terms of what we think we are capable of, and new situations that arise can teach us new things, adding to or updating the information we have on ourselves.

This is also why the process of initiation is so useful. It is designed so that the Initiate is invited to take a journey within, to dig down and truly understand who we are and how we relate to other people. This emphasis on personal inquiry is central to many ancient eastern traditions such as Hinduism and Buddhism, and entire systems of meditation have been designed to allow a person to investigate the apparent facts behind what we experience as the Self and to help lead the practitioner to conclude its true nature.

In meditation, a person spends much of their time training the attention to be mindful of what is going on at this present moment. Whatever is going on consists of what we take in through our five senses as well as the thoughts that arise. The practitioner attempts to merely be aware of what they are conscious of, and to simply let things arise and fall away without getting tied up too much in the thoughts, or whatever has been noticed. Usually, this means that the attention should remain steadily focused on some fixed object, like the movements of the breath. The idea is that if a meditator finds themselves following a particular thought, they should immediately return their attention to their breathing and let the thought fall away on its own. This has the effect of training the attention to be more controllable in any given situation, which also has the side effect of making the meditator more aware of what is going on around them and in their minds.

After some time practising meditation, the practitioner can use meditation to study the activity of their minds, gaining insight into themselves and the true nature of the experience of the Self. This, in many ways, is an essential aspect of initiation; once a Candidate has passed through a stage of initiation and been presented with symbols and their immediate interpretation, they are invited to ruminate on the meaning of their experience. The word for this rumination would be meditation in its broadest sense. There may not be a requirement to sit in contemplation: the Initiate however, might be inclined to learn more from books and other sources to consolidate the meanings of the symbols in their own lives and experience.

Within Freemasonry, the Degree that deals with the Self is the Third Degree, also called the Degree of a Master Mason. In this ceremony, the Masonic Candidate is invited to contemplate the subject of death and what it means to the living of their life. An appreciation of death, rather than being something that should be shied away from, helps to place all of life into perspective. Ordinarily, we pass through life thinking about death as little as possible. However, understanding that life is limited can serve in helping us to understand just how precious life truly is. We all have the opportunity to use our life to the great benefit of many, but we have only limited time to do so: there is, literally, no time like the present.

The Third Degree does not however just concern itself with the awful subject of actual death. It also attempts to symbolise the death of the concept of the Self. Up until the Third Degree the emphasis has been on the Candidate and his progress on the Masonic journey, but in the final Craft Degree the Self is symbolically extinguished and the Initiate is made aware of their wider importance in the world. Once a Candidate undergoes the symbolic demise of the illusory sense of Self they are then shown that they live, by necessity, within a network of fellowship. Once the veil of the illusory Self has slipped away, the wider picture becomes far more apparent.

Freemasonry, as an organisation, also reflects this truth of interdependency in a more general way. One of the rules of a Masonic meeting states that the topics of religion and politics should be avoided in conversation. This is because it is these two subjects, more than any others that serve to divide people. Freemasonry only wishes to focus on those things that all human beings hold in common. It is the recognition of the similarity of all human beings that helps to unite people: to understand that we all suffer the challenges that life presents to us, helping us to feel a bond with other people, and so, perhaps, encouraging us to work towards the alleviation of such suffering.

The Third Degree also effectively mirrors the idea of Dependent Arising. A human being is not a thing that exists in and of itself. The human body is dependent on the physical, chemical, and biological processes that support its physical existence. As has been mentioned, the illusory sense of Self is dependent on the functioning of the brain and its ability to generate the concept as a result of a rational thinking process. Finally, the Third Degree teaches that a human being is dependent on other human beings for their survival.

As has been mentioned previously, human beings must be naturally social animals because of the vulnerable way in which each individual starts life. We require a mother to care for us, then that mother needs the protection and support of the wider group. This group is comprised of many individuals who each have a role in serving that society. For instance, in early societies many of the males would be hunters for the settlement, charged with the acquiring of food, sometimes at the risk of their own lives.

In many of these ancient cultures and even in some that still exist today, initiation rituals were used to teach the young hunter to understand his place in the world. During the initiation process, he would have to face some fearful situation and be able to come through it. Having defeated his fears, he would emerge as a fully-fledged hunter and warrior. This would help ensure that, when feelings of fear presented themselves out in the real world, he would be prepared with the correct psychological tools to deal with them.

In our modern society, we are reliant on many individuals. Everything we do and have requires the involvement of so many of these individuals. For example, simply going to work requires that we travel by car, motorcycle, bus, train or even bicycle, all of which have been built by others and designed by yet more people. The maintenance of these modes of transport requires mechanical specialists, keeping them moving requires people to sell fuel, and yet others to refine that fuel, with still others to source the materials, such as oil, on which that fuel is based.

Of course, all of these aforementioned processes require machinery and technology, and each of these machines and pieces of technology requires people to design and build them. Computer systems used in the various factory processes and offices are designed and built by yet more people, and even the stationery that everyone uses in the support process has to be designed and manufactured. Furthermore, everyone who has worked on the eventual creation of all of these things requires feeding, which requires yet more people. All of this, so you can get to work!

Obviously, the above example has been greatly simplified. If we were to truly analyse all of the people required, we would have many more pages of writing. The number of people required to take part in the support process of you driving to work is phenomenal. Yet this simple example reveals how every individual human being is entirely reliant on others, no matter what we do. It would be very difficult to find any situation that is not reliant on other people.

This truth of interconnectedness further supports the idea that the concept of the individual separate Self is, in fact, an illusion. We cannot find any evidence of an actual Self that isn't simply the result of a thought in the brain. The world that we experience as separate from us is actually the result of impulses going on in the same place that our sense of Self is also generated. And, if we follow the philosophy of Dependent Arising, we will find it hard to accurately think of a kind of existence that is entirely separate from those around us.

However, in the modern world, we are bombarded by the importance of the Self. Our culture seems to place, at the apex of esteem, that which the contemplative traditions take to be a complete illusion. Everything is oriented around the advancement of the Self. The media sets the pace for ambition that is almost entirely designed by the companies who design and produce the products they are trying to sell. Social networks encourage the emphasis on the Self, as people use them to advertise how well their lives are going. A simple glance at the television will eventually show that celebrity can be had at any price, and that people don't even have to have achieved anything to become famous. Modern music is more about the advertisement of the celebrities themselves than conveying any meaningful concept or simply being entertaining. Looked at from the perspective of the very logical concept of Dependent Arising, it would seem that the world has truly lost its way, focusing on the illusory.

To be happy, many people around the world are pursuing the house, the car, the holidays, the restaurants; some even seek fame as well as fortune. Yet all of this would seem to be based around the need to fulfil selfish desires and to feel satisfaction directly from the attainment of these things. However, if we base our happiness around the attainment of material things then we fall into a trap, because material things have limited existence. The cars break down, houses require constant attention to keep them in good order and, eventually, it becomes time to go home from holiday and return to normal life.

Since material possessions are temporary, any sense of lasting happiness that is based on them must be ill-founded. Therefore, it logically follows that lasting happiness must come from some other source, one which can remain as the material things in life ebb and flow. As has been seen, everything that we experience seems to be generated by the impulses in our central nervous system, and this is also true of the emotions. Since happiness is one such emotion, it should be possible to cultivate happiness as a state of mind. Instead of waiting for some external material source to enable us to feel happiness, human beings should be looking for ways in which they can generate the feelings of happiness for themselves.

A favoured way of generating happiness, as expressed by the Eastern contemplative traditions, is through the cultivation of compassion. Compassion is all about relating to others in the full awareness that they are capable of having the full range of emotions that we ourselves have. It is the commitment to generate positive feelings in others or, at the very least, to respect them as living beings.

This is where the philosophy of Dependent Arising comes in useful. If Dependent Arising teaches that each person is reliant on many things and people for existence then it is possible to infer from this that the actions people take are dependent on a variety of causes. This means that no human being acts without some kind of antecedent cause and, no matter if actions are negative or positive, the person who understands the truth of Dependent Arising has insight into the causes of actions and so cannot emphasise the person behaving in a certain way as being the prime cause. Therefore, it becomes impossible to judge others directly, which then leads to a compassionate stance towards other people.

Dependent Arising also teaches us that the actions of one individual can have a massive effect on the world. Imagine you suddenly ceased to exist. What would it take to make the world in which you never existed a reality? Firstly, your parents would not have to have conceived you. Let's imagine, for simplicity, that they never met. To ensure that your parents never met, events would have had to have been different to cause them not to cross paths. Since these events are different, the events that caused these events would have had to have been different, and the events causing these, and so on, going back through a causal chain to the beginning of the universe. Following this logic, it turns out that the conditions of the Big Bang would have to have been slightly different to create a universe in which you never came to be. Yet, everything else in the universe emerged from this same initial event and therefore, should be affected by the initial causes.

In essence, it seems your very existence has an effect on the whole of the universe. It would appear that, because everything exploded into existence from the same source, everything is inextricably interconnected with everything else, regardless of when it existed in the history of the universe. Everything in the universe is dependent on every other thing, so how a person acts in the world will have an effect on everything around them.

Looked at simply, if a person decides to act kindly and with a commitment to make everyone they meet happy, it naturally follows that the people they meet will benefit in some positive way. These people will then be more inclined to act positively towards other people. With enough people acting positively and compassionately towards others, the world begins to transform into a much nicer place to live, the consequence of this being that people will be more predisposed to be happy.

The positive effects that compassionate action has on other people are also reflected within the person performing the acts. When human beings see that they have positively affected the life of another, they are naturally rewarded with a sense of well-being

On a wider perspective, the illusion of the Self being mistaken as real has affected every walk of life, and this is a situation that has existed, pretty much unchanged, since man began to walk the Earth. There are many things that, just like the sense of an individual Self, help to form a separation between the world and others, and there are many other expressions of Self that further divide human beings. One example of this is the idea of borders and countries.

As people, human beings define themselves as being a member of some particular country. This gives a sense of identity for a person that is different from members of another country. Immediately it begins to become easier for people to see themselves as different from each other.

The idea of separate countries also has an effect on the sharing of resources. Anything within the borders of one country is the property of that country, which only they can benefit from. For this reason, many wars and battles have resulted from people from other territories wishing to take over another country, gaining control over their resources. Here, the idea of individuation as expressed in separate nation states has given cause and a reason for people to fight over material possessions.

However, the real truth is that there is not really any such thing as any country one could mention. Effectively, the only way that a geographical country exists is as a concept drawn up on a map showing landmasses. If there is to be any real progress towards a brighter future for all mankind then the idea of borders needs to be revised. In truth, the whole Earth is where human beings live and, because we all share one planet, it doesn't make sense to hold to old-fashioned views of bordered areas of land.

If something were to threaten the Earth then the very notion of separate countries becomes effectively meaningless, because everyone is affected. Examples of this might be a large asteroid, large solar mass ejection, or environmental disaster. However, the last of these potential threats to the Earth, the environmental disaster, is the one that is most immediate for us. Every time chemicals are dumped into the ocean, or belched into the atmosphere, it is the environment that is changed, and everyone on Earth is likely to feel the difference through dying food sources, or changing weather patterns. The fact that all the countries of the Earth are not separate but are, in fact, connected needs to be understood by all governments.

The sharing of resources is also something that could be enabled if the countries of the world were to understand their interdependency. As time goes on, populations go up, and the Earth is only capable of supporting so many in any one place. The concept of separate nations, in this case, is acting as a limiting factor for human progress. Systems need to be set up where the world's resources can be shared more effectively.

Of course, ideas of national borders beginning to blur is already occurring. The United States of America and the European Union are two examples where the need for shared resources has been recognised. That is not to say that these systems don't need improving, they clearly do, but they are certainly a step in the right direction in the recognition of the interdependency of all human beings.

One of the ways that Freemasonry helps to dispel the illusion that people are different from one another is their emphasis on fellowship, with the search for a common truth at the centre of human existence. In order to become a Freemason, a person has to declare a belief in some kind of a supreme being, but the details of individual belief are not questioned. In the concept of deity as the Great Architect of the Universe, Freemasonry has a symbol that each individual Freemason can see as representing their own concept of deity. Similarly, Freemasonry refers to the holy book of any particular religion as simply the Volume of the Sacred Law. Again, this means that when Freemasonry instructs an Initiate to study the Volume of the Sacred Law, that Initiate can understand they are being instructed to study the central scripture of their own faith. From the point of view of religious belief, Freemasonry uses symbolism to imply that all religious and spiritual systems are of equal value.

As the Freemason begins to think symbolically, they will tend to begin to see the world in a different way. In effect, by thinking symbolically, the Freemason's mind is trained in a way of thinking that will enable him to see how the Masonic philosophy can be applied in their own life. Hence, continuing the theme of the similarity of spiritual systems, the

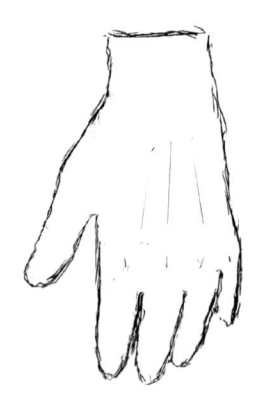

'White Gloves Representing Equality'

Freemason is enabled to see that all of the religions of the world are attempting to understand a transcendent quality underlying the universe, but from different perspectives. The Masonic mind is trained, through initiation, to be able to see the unity inherent in the diversity of cultural systems.

In the chapter on the Second Degree, it was seen that the level symbolises equality. Another symbol that Freemasonry uses to denote equality comes from a part of how Freemasons dress. Along with their ordinary dark suits and apron, Freemasons wear white gloves. This, too, denotes equality amongst Freemasons. No matter what a Freemason does in life, whether they have the rough hands of a builder or carpenter, or the smooth hands of a lawyer or a banker, everyone is considered equal. The white gloves do the job of placing everyone, no matter what there station in life, on an equal standing.

Equality is also expressed in the organisation of the Masonic system. Within Freemasonry there are the officers of the lodge, and there are also members of Provincial Grand Lodges and Grand Lodge. As a general rule, the Provincial Lodges around the country help to govern the lodges in their respective jurisdictions, with Grand Lodge governing the Provincial Lodges. However, the hierarchical systems of the world at large are not reflected in Freemasonry. The officers of a lodge are not considered superior to other Brethren who hold more junior positions, and the officers of a Provincial Grand Lodge are not considered superior to the officers of a standard lodge, even though they have been promoted to a position in Provincial Grand Lodge some time after their term as Master of their own lodge. This also follows through to Grand Lodge, where the members are not considered superior to those officers in Provincial and standard lodges. Members of Grand Lodge and Provincial Grand Lodge are honoured and recognised in a Masonic context, but only to mark their progress in and experience of Freemasonry.

In a similar way, Freemasonry doesn't recognise hierarchies that are taken for granted in the non-Masonic world. For instance, if a prince of a country is a Freemason then, technically, their position in society does not hold sway in the context of Freemasonry. Whether one is a prince or a labourer, Freemasons consider each other brothers in Freemasonry first and foremost. In the context of the non-Masonic world, of course,

Masonic brothers treat each other as titles might suggest, so the prince is once again treated as a prince.

This emphasis on equality within Freemasonry helps the Mason to take this quality out into the world. With so much focus on all members of a lodge being equal, the Freemason is encouraged to view everyone as equals. Just as Freemasonry honours progress through Masonry as something to be recognised, without emphasising any superiority, the Freemason should view people according to their merits.

The emphasis on equality is obviously intended to make the Masonic Candidate see how everyone is equal, and this is helped by combining it with a study of the Self. As the idea of the Self as an entity that exists in and of itself begins to fall away, the Masonic Candidate also understands their own mind better. After knocking away the surplus material to uncover that which lies within, the Freemason has a better view of who they are, along with an honest appraisal of what it means to be human, with all of their fears placed in full view of the mind.

In the knowledge that every human being is equal, the natural conclusion is that every human being is subject to the same doubts, fears and general suffering. Therefore, by taking the teachings of Freemasonry together and by understanding one's own plight, one also acquires a kind of direct understanding of the plight of every other human being. This has the effect of encouraging a genuine sense of compassion towards others.

Compassion is the light that reveals the truth of interdependency, and this truth is further driven home by the emphasis on charity. Freemasonry gives large quantities of money to good causes around the world annually. In the course of Masonic initiation, charity is described as the distinguishing quality of a Freemason's heart. Whenever someone is found to be in need, the Freemason is encouraged to do whatever they can to help. This idea of charity is not restricted to money; aid, after all, can be given in terms of one's time and skills.

It is the overall aim of Freemasonry to create a better world, and the concept of initiation is key to this endeavour. Initiation is about making a beginning. When a Masonic Candidate enters the lodge for the first time, and just before they are initiated, the door closes on the life they once had. When they step out of that lodge room after that first meeting they have become a new person, one who has pledged to live the rest of their lives by Masonic principles. This is different to simply joining a club, as joining a club is just a continuation of one's life but with an extra membership added to it. Initiation is intended to make the joining of Freemasonry a profound experience, and one that changes a person.

As the Freemason continues on their journey of initiation and progresses, they become a craftsman of themselves. They seek the truth of themselves by exploring their own inner lives and minds. The working-tools of each of the Degrees encourages the Mason to focus more on their daily conduct, to become aware of the reasons they behave the way they do and, if their behaviour falls below the high standards they have set for themselves, to alter their behaviour accordingly.

Being aware of the thoughts, emotions and behaviour that arise in the course of one's day-to-day experience, as has been mentioned above, is known as mindfulness. The idea of mindfulness is to be aware of what is going on, moment to moment, within one's own mind, and therefore to better understand one's own behaviour. Many of us move through life in a constant state of stimulus-response. Things happen to us, one thing after another, with us responding to what happens immediately, most of the time without any thought as to our actions; we tend to act on the basis of our instincts more than we think we do.

However, becoming ever-aware of the changing quality of experience and how one is responding to it automatically creates a gap between receiving a stimulus and responding to it. By taking the time to ask themselves what is the best way to respond to a given situation, the Freemason gives themselves the choice of acting according to higher principles than instinct might recommend. For instance, a person might become angry in any given situation, but if that person allows themselves the time to observe the emotion of anger rising in the mind and body then it gives them a chance to consider the consequences of actions or words fuelled by anger. Once these outcomes have been looked at there is then time to take into consideration moral principles that will help in the choosing of a response that benefits as many people as possible. By the time all of this has happened, the person who initially became angry will find that the emotion has completely reduced in severity, or ebbed away completely. That person is then free to respond in an entirely rational way, not governed by negative emotion.

Emotions that arise in the body and mind are only fuelled if the mind is allowed to be carried along by them. Observing emotions and then taking time to rationally think through responses takes the focus off the effects of the emotion itself. Since the conscious mind is only capable of focusing on one thing at a time, negative emotions quickly lose momentum in a mind that has found a way to step back and observe when they occur and to focus on solutions.

Through mindfulness, the Freemason chips away at the metaphorical stone that symbolises their own inner Self. As they discover parts of their mind that do not behave according to higher principles they focus on improving this part of their personality, as if knocking away a piece of stone that does not conform to the intended form.

Eventually, the journey of the Freemason results in a mind that has been trained to act in accordance with morality. Alongside this, the focus on the Self has revealed that there exists a mysterious quality of the mind that appears to transcend rational understanding. This of course, is the mysterious quality of experience itself.

Yet, even though the knowledge of themselves has been greatly improved, the Freemason soon discovers that the very nature of the Self is indeed a figment generated in dependence on other things, that the individual cannot exist without other people, and that, truly, no person is an island. The focus then shifts from the ideals of the morally improved mind to the subject of how this mind can be used to serve others.

Having been crafted by the process of initiation and years of studying the nature of themselves, the Freemason understands the value of conducting their life according to Masonic principles. By conducting their affairs according to the highest virtues, their behaviour becomes beneficial to everyone that the Freemason meets. If each Freemason continues to act in this way, a lot of good extends into the world along the lines of interconnectedness that inextricably binds us all together.

CHAPTER 9

THE TRANSFORMATIVE SYMBOLISM OF THE ROYAL ARCH

'The interlaced triangles of the Royal Arch,
representing the union of man with the divine'

No work on Freemasonry is complete without some description of what is known as the Holy Royal Arch, which is most often just called the Royal Arch. Although it is presented to the Freemason as a separate ceremony of Freemasonry and appears to be distinct from the other Three Degrees of what is usually known as Craft Freemasonry, the Royal Arch is not, in fact, a separate Degree but rather the completion of the Third Degree.

At one time, the Royal Arch formed part of the Third Degree ceremony. However, it was decided that it would be best to detach the Ceremony of Exaltation – as the Royal Arch portion of Masonic initiation is called – and turn it into a ceremony in its own right, because it tended to unnecessarily extend the ceremony of initiating the Master Mason. Also, because the officers and furniture involved in the Exaltation Ceremony are different, it required the entire lodge room to be re-arranged every time the relevant stage of the Third Degree ceremony was reached.

The journey in stone of the Freemason finds its conclusion in the Third Degree and has, as its subject, the awful subject of death and how it should be dealt with in the course of one's life. As has been already mentioned in the previous chapter, not only does the Degree of the Master Mason cover the reality of physical death, it also symbolises the physical death of the Self, and the resurrection to a life in which the Freemason is aware of the necessary interconnectedness of the whole of society.

The Ceremony of Exaltation in the Royal Arch then further emphasises the lessons taught in the Third Degree and elaborates on them further. In many ways, the Royal Arch is the most mystical part of Masonic initiation. Some might suggest that the other Degrees in Masonry, for example those in the Scottish Rite, also have a mystical content, but it is worth remembering here that the Degrees beyond the Royal Arch tend to further illustrate the points made in the three original Degrees of the Craft, and are not necessary for the completion of Masonic initiation.

What the Royal Arch deals with is the mystical qualities that underlie consciousness. Its theme is that it is indeed possible to unite with these qualities in order to acquire further insight into the nature of existence. For this reason, the Royal Arch is often seen as the capstone of Freemasonry, i.e. that part of initiation that concludes and explains its true purpose. Indeed, the Royal Arch is sometimes called 'Chapter' from the word 'Chapter', which is a piece of masonry atop a free-standing pillar.

At the beginning of the Ceremony of Exaltation the Candidate is understood to have undergone the process of dying to the Self in the Third Degree, and it is at this point that the Royal Arch takes over to further illustrate the lessons of that Degree.

It is also important to point out the context of the story in which the Ceremony of Exaltation is set. Whereas the story of the Three Degrees of Craft Masonry are assumed to be set in the times of the building of the first Temple of Jerusalem, the setting for the story of the Royal Arch is the period of history after Jerusalem was sacked by the Babylonian King Nebuchadnezzar II. At this point, King Solomon's original temple lies in ruins, and the Israelites are living in exile in Babylon.

However, in the Ceremony of Exaltation, the Candidate represents someone who returns from exile, and discovers the ruined temple.

It is worth remembering at this point that one of the many things that King Solomon's Temple symbolises is the microcosm, or the individual human being. Therefore, the ruined temple represents the broken individual, or a person who has died, as in the Third Degree. This death, as has been pointed out, is not an actual physical death, but the death of what the Freemason initially took for granted as a sense of an independent, separate Self.

In the story of the Ceremony of Exaltation the exile who has returned, represented by the Candidate, finds what appears to be a dome-like structure protruding from the ground where the Temple once stood. Upon tapping it, it sounds as though it is hollow. Out of curiosity, the exile decides that, with the help of some companions, he is going to remove the stones of this dome to discover what is underneath.

The intrepid exile is then lowered into the dark vault below in order to discover what is down there. This lowering into the darkness of the Earth is itself of symbolic significance for the Candidate for Exaltation: the Initiate is symbolically being lowered into the dark recesses of himself, or his own subconscious.

The symbolic death of the Third Degree has taken away the focus on external material things, and all senses are now focused within. This is very similar to the meditative exercises alluded to in the previous chapter. With practice, the focus of conscious attention in meditation can be trained to block out all distractions from the outside world as well as the processes of ordinary conscious thought, and the meditator is then said to be left with the peaceful state of pure being.

Once in this state of pure being, a person only sees the emptiness of Self. There is only the darkness marking the absence of all sense and thought impressions. However, although thoughts and senses have been excluded from consciousness it becomes glaringly obvious that there still appears to be this sense of Self that is watching in the darkness. This helps the meditator to come to the conclusion that their sense of Self is not associated with the contents of their conscience, but is something different.

Although the Freemason who has undergone the Ceremony of Exaltation does not necessarily meditate to ponder the mysteries of its symbolism, it is nevertheless necessary to contemplate the meaning of Exaltation over time in one's own mind.

Once the nature of the Self has been analysed so all that is left is the experience of simply being conscious, the attention then naturally turns to the nature of conscious experience itself.

The nature of conscious experience is indeed a mysterious thing. Whilst neuroscientists are capable of understanding, which neurons in the brain light up when we look at or listen to something, there is nothing in modern science that can sufficiently explain what conscious experience actually is. An example, which we have used before, is the experience of colour. We have no idea what the experience of red, blue, or any other colour actually is. Science provides answers, such as the fact that each colour is a particular wavelength of light, but this merely describes the nature of light, not the nature of the experience of colour.

When light enters our eyes it stimulates cells on the retina, which send electrochemical impulses into the brain. The brain then interprets the signals and conjures up the experience of the relevant colour. However, there is nothing that explains what happens to turn neuronal impulses into the quality of actual experience.

Another way of looking at this is to imagine a picture of a tree. Any scientist could hook you up to a functional MRI scan and establish which neurons are correlated with the image of the tree that is currently in your mind's eye. However, they cannot see the actual picture of the tree that you are experiencing. Even if the scientist opened up your skull and looked through your brain to find evidence of the tree in your mind, they would not find it. Where, then, is the tree you are seeing?

The answer to this question seems to be impossible to answer, and, it is difficult to say whether science will ever find an answer to this particular conundrum. This aspect of experience may indeed be of such a nature as to truly transcend human understanding. It is possible, though, to know where the answer does in fact lie. Although we could never be able to confirm it, simple logic can confirm the whereabouts of the answer to all experience.

Before answering the question of where the ground of experience lies, we need to return to the idea that the existence of the universe also rests on principles that transcend human understanding. However, although the ground of all existence is beyond human conception, it still is the transcendent origin of all things, including the way that experience functions. This then is where our answer lies.

The meaning of this is very profound. It essentially means that the transcendent nature, which is the origin of all existence, is one with the origin of all experience. This has been the intention of mystical systems throughout history. Despite the ordinary disciplines of any of the world's religions, they always contain an inner core that speaks of the union between man and God. An example of this is Gnosticism, which existed around the time of Jesus. The philosophy of Gnosticism centred around the idea that existence was an entrapment of what they regarded as the soul, which was in fact a portion of the divine spark. The goal of spiritual discipline, then, was to seek oneness with the divine and to ascend out of the prison of the flesh. The important thing to recognise here, though, is that the Self was thought to be divine in nature.

Gnosticism is not alone in this philosophy, as the Jewish mystical system of Kabbalah teaches that God created the universe by a process of emanations from His divine source and that all things are direct expressions and components of the divine. The mystical aspect of Islam, Sufism, also centres around the idea that human beings and God are one, and in Hinduism there is said to be no essential difference between the personal soul, Atman, and the world soul, Brahman. The idea that the human Self and the transcendent origin of all things merge and are indeed one has echoed throughout history. In fact, the reason initiation exists is to bring an Initiate into direct knowledge of this. Only through personal exploration of the inner psychology can one uncover the truth.

To mirror this insight, in the Ceremony of Exaltation the Candidate, symbolically groping around in the dark of an underground vault, discovers something, and what that something is symbolised by a scroll on which are written passages of the Volume of the Sacred Law. In other words, by exploring the deep and dark recesses of pure consciousness the divine spark within is discovered.

To emphasise further what has been discovered, something else is found within the vault: the inscription of the name of God. To give this its historical context, the name of God, for the Israelites, whose temple it was, was so holy that it could never be uttered. This in itself can be regarded as a symbol that comes straight out of the Hebrew Bible. It could be conjectured that the reason the name of God was not to be pronounced was the same reason that the face of God could not be looked upon by human eyes: it is a representation of the unknowable quality of the course of all things. God cannot be looked upon because the transcendent source cannot be apprehended by human reason, and the name of God (in other words, the description of the deity) cannot be expressed for the same reason.

Nevertheless, this artefact, symbolising the divine within, is discovered in the deep underground recesses of the first temple at Jerusalem, representing the deepest part of the Self.

Once the artefact, the sacred symbol, has been discovered, the Candidate is then symbolically pulled out of the dark vault of the subterranean part of the temple and rejoins his companions. This act alone is symbolic of the fact that the Initiate, having found what is within the depths of himself, then brings the knowledge of it out of the darkness and into the light of day. In other words, rather than the knowledge of the union between the Self and the transcendent remaining in the obscurity and depths of his subconscious, he has brought it into the light of consciousness.

The knowledge of the presence of this principle within should effect an interesting transformation. Once the Candidate understands that it is the transcendent within that connects them with the transcendent in all other things, a new sense of purpose is found. They are enabled to understand that they are an essential element in existence, and that fulfilling their purpose to the fullest extent for the benefit of the wider world is now their goal.

This can be represented by the combination of the square and compasses, which we have visited before. At the beginning of a Mason's journey the compasses are hidden beneath the square. In other words, the divine symbolised by the circle is hidden within the coarser material Self, represented by the square. In the Third Degree, both legs of the compasses are exposed and rest above the square, meaning that the divine circle is now outside the more material square.

This means that Freemasons express themselves according to the grander scheme. However, rather than necessarily needing to refer to the Volume of the Sacred Law to understand what that wider scheme is, the Initiate is in a position to understand that, by virtue of their connection with the transcendent, they can understand how to express themselves to be of best service.

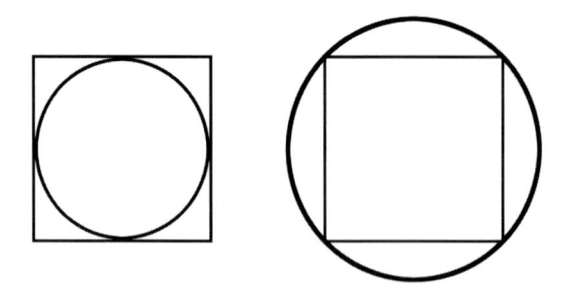

'The Divine (The Circle) is Discovered within the Material (The Square) and Expressed'

In a way, the light, which has been found within, is illuminating their conscious mind. It is as if the crafting of initiation has cleared away the rubble and unnecessary material which was obscuring its rays for so long.

The loss of the sense of a separate Self is also created once the unity with the transcendent is discovered. Since it is the same principle that lies at the foundation of everything in existence, it can no longer be accepted that the Self is an entity separate and distinct from everything else. It becomes clear that there is, in fact, only one cohesive whole expressed as the cosmos.

Looked at from a scientific perspective, this does make perfect sense. Physicists and cosmologists continue to look for the mathematical principles which underlie what we see as the universe. This is not to be confused with the transcendent origin we have already spoken about. Instead, we are talking about the mathematical framework that describes the initial conditions of the Big Bang, and which therefore underlies everything that exists. If this unified principle exists, it would mean that, no matter how distinct and separate things seem to be in the universe, because these things are governed by one principle everything must proceed as one system.

Each part of the universal system evolves according to a singular principle which governs everything. Realising this, the Initiate knows that the boundaries between themselves and everything else melt away. And, as a consequence of this dissolving of borders, other things promoted and taught in Freemasonry automatically fall into place. The Initiate, knowing what it is like to be themselves, can understand what it is like to be every human being. The borders having fallen away, it is logically understood that all of humankind are actually one, as if possessing one mind and one body. The exalted Initiate begins to regard the whole of humankind as they would their own body, and true compassion towards all human beings is achieved.

The Initiate who has completed the Third Degree, including the insights afforded in the Royal Arch, now feels that they want to actively do everything they can to ensure the ongoing health of the organism of mankind as a whole, understanding that every member of its population is precious and necessary, or else they wouldn't have come into existence as a result of the universal guiding principle.

The unification of the Self with the spark of the transcendent within is, as has been explained, the purpose of the Royal Arch initiation ceremony. However, rather than a unification, it is to be seen as more of a re-unification. If we remember the exile who has come from Babylon, and who originally had his home in Jerusalem, where heaven met Earth through the temple, then the process is all about a return after a long absence. This, in itself, is symbolic of the plight of existence. The expulsion to Babylon and the return to the temple ruins only to discover a holy secret symbolise the spiritual journey of life. We are all born into this world, and are educated about the world, but we have come into existence as a natural consequence of the transcendent principle behind all things: our origin is in the transcendent.

In life, we wander through the confusion of the world, trying to understand the world around us, whilst trying to do our best to live a good life. This is akin to the time the exile spent in Babylon. However, the exile then returns from Babylon to the ruined temple where they make their discovery. In other words, through the process of initiation and contemplation, the Freemason leaves the confusion of the world to look deep within themselves, only to discover the transcendent secret within: the Initiate comes home to the transcendent.

This same story is played out in the Biblical story of Adam and Eve. This story represents the expulsion of humanity from the transcendent to a life of toil and suffering. Then, through steady progress, the eventual destiny of mankind is to reunite with the transcendent.

Having experienced the world and attained a unifying knowledge with the transcendent through initiation, a use can be found for such an experience. Since divine knowledge is contained within the living Initiate, they can share the benefits of this knowledge with the rest of the world through their words and actions.

The form of a Masonic chapter, as we have mentioned, is different from that of a Masonic lodge, and the officers are also different. Even so, just as in the Craft Lodge, each of the officers has a symbolic import. In the Royal Arch, there are nine main officers. The first of these are the Three Sojourners who, in the story, arrive from Babylon and return to the temple. The Principal Sojourner is the position filled by the Candidate for Exaltation. It is this intrepid fellow who descends into the darkness to discover a secret. Hence, this Sojourner represents the faculty of consciousness, i.e. that quality we use to explore the inner recesses of our mind. The two Assistant Sojourners are the ones who symbolically lower the Candidate into the darkness. Rather than letting him fall, they hold him by a lifeline as he explores the innermost darkness. These two officers represent rationality and intelligence, without which we would be lost in our own search into our psyche. We can only obtain anything of value in introspection if we remain grounded in reason. These two Assistant Sojourners are also responsible for lifting the Candidate back out of the darkness and into the light of day.

This trio of Sojourners represent the material aspect of the human being: they enter the chapter room from the West to approach the East, where the light of wisdom emanates. Opposing them, sat in the East, are the Three Principals, the primary of whom is Zerubbabel.

Zerubbabel represents the polar opposite of the Principal Sojourner. Whereas the Principal Sojourner comes from the confusion of the world, ready to discover the divine principle awaiting him, the Prince of the People represents the higher principle from which the human being can act, once consciousness has been enlightened by the rays of divine wisdom.

Just as the Principal Sojourner has his opposite in the East, so too do the Assistant Sojourners in the guise of Haggai the prophet, and Joshua the High Priest.

Haggai, being a prophet, represents that spiritual aspect in man that seems to indicate there is something more that is lying deep down inside. It is this feeling that has inspired many people over thousands of years to seek out the deeper meaning to existence. Human beings have always known there is more to understand, some truth to uncover that will help us understand our origin and purpose.

Of course, there is no guarantee that, just because we are looking for it, there is anything to be discovered. However, despite this fact, we have an almost instinctual impulse to understand. It is as if we feel the presence of some great truth but are unable to discern what it is or how to find it.

This feeling has been almost entirely responsible for the advancement of human beings. Mystics have sought out the hidden mysteries of the Self and, in some cases, have inspired the creation of entire religions which allow others to follow the same path. Artists, feeling that there is something deep down within, and within the fabric of the world, have sought a variety of ways in which it might be expressed through creative endeavour. Philosophers have spent thousands of years using their faculty of reason and the intellect to try to find and express this truth. In fact, the Father of Philosophy, Socrates, thought that the truth was so subtle and difficult to understand that he developed his method of questioning everything until the truth was uncovered.

In recent times, over the last few hundred years, it has been scientists who have attempted to answer the call of this illusive truth, to uncover it through direct observation and logical analysis.

To summarise, Haggai the prophet foreshadows the presence of a principle deep within, which we have yet to find.

Joshua, the high priest, represents the connection between the material part of us and the divine aspect of us. The usual job of a priest is to mediate between the divine and the lower human being. This office represents the faculty of human nature that follows the guidance of the transcendent source. This might be be understood as the human ability to listen to – or, alternatively, completely ignore – gut-feeling and instinct. Sometimes we simply know what we need to do: we don't know how we know, but there seems to be something within us, urging us on. Often, our sense of fear takes over, and we choose not to follow our gut feeling in favour of rationality and what we already know.

It should be remembered, however, that animals all work on instinct at its most basic level, and manage to survive. Human beings, also, have managed to survive from very ancient times, and so have been able to pass down those survival instincts to us, their descendants. Perhaps, then, we should trust our instincts, as represented by Joshua, more often.

In between the Sojourners in the West and the Principals in the East, we have the two Scribes Nehemiah and Ezra. Nehemiah can be found in the South-West of the chapter, and represents the Candidate's progress as they attempt to rebuild themselves from the confused state afforded them from wandering the world. Through the progress of Craft Masonry, the Principal Sojourner has crafted and built themselves in accordance with the principle of Masonic initiation. In the Northeast of the chapter sits Ezra, the Chief Scribe, who is placed nearer to the Three Principals representing the aspects of spirituality; it is Ezra who represents the more advanced progress towards the transcendent wisdom represented by the East.

Remembering that Ezra and Nehemiah are scribes, it should be understood that they represent the recording of the spiritual progress that the Initiate has made. It is only through the recording of memory that anything is learned and so, as the Masonic Initiate makes discoveries, those discoveries are recorded in order to mark their progress and to inspire further research.

The ninth office is that of the Janitor who, like the Tyler of the Craft lodge, guards the door of the chapter room from those who might wish to gain entry. The Janitor symbolises the connection between the inner world and the outer world. It is through the Janitor that the benefits of Exaltation will pass. Yet it is also this facility that guards against anything from the outside world that might hinder the progress of the Initiate.

The whole ceremony of exaltation was once part of the Third Degree ceremony, and so it is important to bear in mind the overall context of this phase of the Masonic initiation process. When the Initiate, having searched in the darkness of symbolic death, is raised out of the darkness to the realisation of the interconnectedness of all of society and the truths of human fellowship they bring with them a great secret that can now be used to guide their life in the service of others.

If one was to look at Craft Masonry on its own, without the Royal Arch aspect, it would seem that Freemasonry is simply about the understanding of morality and how it can help the Freemason progress through life, doing the best they can to promote a better society, and finding how they can best be of service. This, in itself is quite enough for an institution to impart. However, it is the Royal Arch aspect of the process of initiation that finally explains why the progress of Freemasonry is seen as having what can be called a more spiritual aspect.

Indeed, the profound discovery in the Royal Arch has the effect of redefining – whilst at the same time explaining – the system of Masonic initiation. It is therefore useful to revisit the whole system of initiation set within the context of the mystical aspects revealed by the Royal Arch.

From the very beginning, the new Initiate enters the life of a Freemason with all of the roughness of a stone freshly cut from the quarry. They are introduced to a system of initiation that will help them craft themselves into a more useful member of society.

Deep within, the Initiate perhaps feels there is something to be known, some deeper mystery which they understand is there, but can't quite get at. Therefore, the symbolic cutting away of the rough parts of themselves is the perfect metaphor for journeying within to find the secret of their being.

Their first encounter with Freemasonry is the First Degree where they are introduced to the whole system of Freemasonry and what it expects of its members. The new Candidate is informed that the life of a Mason is one where the main goal is the pursuit of the highest moral standards. To help them begin their contemplative journey they are given the first set of working-tools, namely the twenty-four inch gauge, the common gavel, and the chisel. The twenty-four inch gauge defines how they are to live their lives: some of it spent being of useful service through their work, part in attending to the needs of others when they are in need, and part of it with their focus squarely on their conception of the transcendent.

This is the first time the Initiate is invited to contemplate anything approaching the spiritual; the second occasion is when they are invited to investigate their conception of the Volume of the Sacred Law. In the context of the ultimate revelation in the Royal Arch, the transcendent is clearly a major focus that is foreshadowed throughout the First Degree.

In fact, the Candidate for initiation first encounters the possibility that Freemasonry might have some kind of spiritual context when they are asked if they believe in a supreme being of some description. It is never questioned what kind of supreme being the Candidate believes in. This simple question, at interview, tells us two things. One is that there must be some emphasis on spiritual belief within the system of Freemasonry, while the other is that it doesn't seem to matter what conception of the spiritual one has so long as one has one, meaning there is perhaps an underlying theme threading through all spiritual traditions which Freemasonry will focus on.

The common gavel represents the Initiate's conscience. It is this faculty that the Freemason should use to guide them through life and in their conduct with other people. The idea of using the force of conscience is to ensure that the activity of the mind is kept under rigid discipline so that nothing negative pollutes the thought process. This is a way of purifying the mind by purifying one's thoughts.

Ensuring that the Candidate works on banishing any unbecoming thoughts that he might have regarding his actions or about other people prepares them for the moment when they will eventually discover that their previously held idea of a separate Self melts into the oneness of all humanity. The Initiate is then prepared to open their mind to the needs of the community around them.

The chisel symbolises education, which helps to further refine the character and intellect of the Candidate. The journey of the Freemason is one that requires analysis and rationality, as well as an understanding of the deeper emotions. To assist with this, the intelligence and rationality are exercised through the acquisition and application of knowledge. The greater the amount of knowledge about the world that the Freemason has, the more their innate sense of wisdom will begin to flourish. They will begin to understand the innate interconnectedness of all of the systems of the world and, eventually, will be able to trace them to their ultimate origin, which will eventually be revealed to them in the Ceremony of Exaltation.

Once some time has been spent as a First Degree, or Entered Apprentice Freemason, the time comes for them to embark on the second leg of their journey, called the Fellow Craft, or Second Degree. The emphasis for this Degree turns from the essential processes of self-crafting as presented in the First Degree to the process of measurement. What is meant by measurement for the Freemason is constant reflection on where they are in their moral development. To help illustrate this inner measurement, actual measuring-tools from the stonemasons guilds are used. They are the square, level and plumb rule.

The square teaches the basic quality of morality. The Freemason is encouraged to do to others what they would have done to them, which is also known as Square Conduct. In order to do this, an awareness is required that the inner qualities of other people are essentially the same as their own. Once again, the idea of an essential thread running through all of humanity is foreshadowed here.

The level takes the lessons of the square a little further. The level represents the sense of equality which the Freemason should feel with the rest of the world, i.e. that all human beings are essentially equal. As the Freemason moves through their ordinary lives, they will see that there is indeed a wide variety of differences all around in terms of race, gender, intellect and ability, to name but four. The Freemason is therefore invited to look beyond surface differences to the qualities that everyone shares, regardless of their obvious differences. This is an opportunity to discover the essential human spirit that lives within all of us, which has the potential to overcome the challenges of the differentiated material world.

The plumb rule teaches the lesson of uprightness in thought and action, which means that mindfulness of one's own mind must be maintained so that the aspirations of the Freemason, from a moral standpoint, are always focused on the highest virtues. This requires the Freemason to be aware that the inner temptations to take the short-cuts in life are ever-present, and that they should always maintain the resolve to act according to higher principles. From the point of view of the mystical aspect of Freemasonry, this helps to train the Initiate to activate that intangible principle within that flows from some higher source, rather than the baser desires of the human animal.

As well as the working-tools, the Second Degree emphasises the need to study the hidden mysteries of nature and science. Therefore, at this stage in the initiation process, the Freemason is required to analyse more specifically the laws that underpin the universe so they can begin to understand that there is a commonality and interconnectedness to it all. Knowledge of science and nature that alludes to the commonality of all things can usually be found in mathematics, where constants such as the Golden Mean and Pi are to be found everywhere.

It is no coincidence that geometry is the overall theme of the Second Degree. Geometry originally comes from the Greek, meaning 'Earth measurement.' However, our understanding of geometry is the idea that complex systems can be reduced to simpler terms. From a mystical point of view, this is exactly what Freemasonry attempts to do: to take the various aspects of the world, and lead the Initiate back through the paths of a kind of spiritual geometry to the source of all things.

Also, within the Second Degree, the journey of the Mason is illustrated by the winding staircase. As they travel on their journey, they are moving upwards and inwards to the middle chamber. This is clearly foreshadowing the approach to the divine source of all things. The upward journey represents that the Initiate is moving from the realm of the material to the heavens with which the divine is traditionally associated. All the while this journey is ascending to the transcendent it is also journeying inwards to a middle chamber within a temple that has been seen to represent not only society as a whole but the individual human being. Furthermore, within that middle chamber can be found the place where the transcendent meets the Earth in the Holy of Holies.

The mystical end-point of the journey of the Freemason is very clear here. It implies that the Freemason is aspiring to higher and higher virtues, bringing them into a wider view of the world and its interconnectedness, whilst at the same time journeying to a place within their deepest core where one can find the abode of the spark of the transcendent origin that infuses all things with existence and life.

This is further alluded to when the Initiate enters the Third Degree. The overall theme of this Master Mason's Degree is finding that which was lost: this is taken to be our oneness with the transcendent, which has been lost for many thousands of years within the confusion of material existence. The secrets to be found are called the genuine secrets of a Master Mason.

In the story of the Freemason, these genuine secrets were lost when the principal architect of King Solomon's Temple met his untimely death. Since the genuine secrets were lost, substitute ones have replaced them, which comprise the methods of recognition between Freemasons. These substitute secrets, however, are meant to remind the Freemason that there are genuine secrets to be found, and that it is the job of all Freemasons to seek them out.

To point the Freemason in the right direction, the Third Degree offers a clue as to where the genuine secrets can be found: within the centre. Quite clearly, this points the seeker to the core of themselves and foreshadows what is to come in the third and final part of pure Craft initiation.

To aid with their further contemplation, the Candidate for the Third Degree is given more symbolic tools to work with: these are the skirret, the pencil, and the compasses. All of these tools refer to the wider plan.

From the vantage point of the Royal Arch Initiate, the wider plan can be apprehended once the concept of the separate Self has been melted away by the revealing light of the transcendent source within them. However, the Freemason passing through the Third Degree initiation ceremony is informed that they should try to align their actions with the principles they find through the Volume of the Sacred Law.

It is a well-known phenomenon that when reading a book, or listening to a speaker, it is sometimes possible to find that insights can be revealed from what is being heard. The insight is usually accompanied by a feeling deep down, as if something has stirred your very essence. It is not necessarily the words which have been taken in that are the source of this profound feeling. It appears to be something between the words, a certain subtext that is presenting itself to the reader. Not everyone experiencing the same words will acquire this insight. It is as if the insight can only be experienced by those who have had sufficient experience and prior understanding to discern it.

This phenomenon is what, it is hoped, will be aroused in the Masonic Initiate by directing their attention to the Volume of the Sacred Law. From the experience afforded them by the particulars of initiation and a contemplative mind, the hidden truths in the subtext of the volume might shine forth for their discernment.

It should be remembered that the holy books of the world have been compiled by, or inspired by, people who have had the profound experience of oneness with the transcendent. This profound experience has been understood in different ways by each of the individuals: for some, Angels visited them and brought the word of God, for others, it was a visitation by the divine on a mountain-top, for others still, revelation came to them after baptism. The experience of union with the transcendent has been interpreted in so many ways because each of those who experience it has a different mind-set. These different mind-sets are the result of different upbringings in different parts of the world, with different cultural traditions.

After the experience of unification has occurred, it leaves the person in a state of profound peace and understanding, and the first thing they want to do is to share it. They tell select groups of people who might be chosen based on their capacity to understand such things, or they tell whoever will listen, or they write it down. The problem with all this is that the experience cannot be put into words. In the attempt to codify the profundity of experience, allegories and proverbs must be utilised, for words are simply not enough. In Masonic terms, the verbal structures and words are symbolic substitutes for the genuine secrets they are attempting to express.

However, since it was the revelation of the transcendent which inspires such writings, those studying the text with the eyes to see may discern the profound secret for themselves and feel the stirring of their cores. It is the point of initiation to prepare a Candidate for such an insight.

The skirret, then, points out the conduct a Freemason should engage in with respect to those around him, as can be found in their conception of the Volume of the Sacred Law. Regardless of what kinds of conduct appear in the actual words of the text, an allegorical reading will yield a humanitarian message, one which unites humankind rather than divides it.

The pencil reminds the Third Degree Freemason that the transcendent origin of the world monitors their actions. It does this, from the core of the world where it resides, through the power of the conscience, which is symbolised by the common gavel in the First Degree. The workings of the conscience are guided by the logical principles that emanate from the transcendent core of being that animates every cell of our bodies. Therefore, when we feel the watchful eye of our conscience guiding us through our actions it can be seen as the guiding principle of the transcendent. This function of guidance is also symbolised by the high priest, Joshua, in the Royal Arch ceremony, as mentioned above.

Whenever we put a foot wrong we remember it, and our conscience is aware of it, and judges whether or not those past actions were aligned with the highest principles. Where they are not, the instinct in our cores lets us know, so that our future actions can be different and more aligned with grander principles.

The compasses help to teach the Third Degree Initiate that rewards will come from correct action, and punishment from incorrect or morally reprehensible action. For many this might imply that those who are good are rewarded in heaven, and those who are bad are punished in a kind of hell. This is not what the message of the compasses is, however: the rewards and punishments come in this life.

Correct conduct that is aligned with the conscience, as derived from the core of being, has a tendency to bring one closer to that core. Just as the core can be felt when insight is experienced which aligns with it, so too can it be felt when actions are performed which also align with it. In fact, the more often dealings with others are in alignment with the guidance from within, and the more often the results of those actions are seen as time evolves, then the deeper is the understanding and the more profound the insight that can be acquired into the fundamental workings of the world. Indeed, subtler influences, not always clear in the world, can sometimes come to the attention of an observer through such insight.

Just like the Mason when they reach the top of the symbolic winding staircase and enter the middle chamber of the temple to receive their reward, the person who listens to their conscience and acts accordingly approaches the reward of becoming one with the source and the core of being and, from here, all things are possible.

The punishment alluded to for those who do not adhere to a line of moral conduct is a slipping further away from the union with the source. The confusion of the world around us will have a tendency to swallow a person up and carry them along with it unless they are able to feel the guiding principles within. The more one slips into the confusion of the world, the slighter the feeling inside becomes, and the more difficult it is to find it again.

After passing through the Craft Degrees and working with the tools and other symbols therein the Freemason, if they have studied carefully, will be fully prepared to discover the genuine secrets of the Master Mason, which are nothing less than the source of all life and wisdom. However, before they can do this, they must withdraw from the material world and journey within and to the centre, where these secrets lie. Therefore, in the Third Degree the Candidate is required to experience a symbolic death representing this withdrawal.

Knowing that their heart and mind have been prepared by the journey of Masonic initiation, they trust that they will know what they are looking for when they find it. The mind, having been prepared, guides them to alight on the discovery of the secret, and upon union with the transcendent at the core of all things. Understanding this, they are raised to where their companions await and realise that they are truly one with all of them, because they all have this same transcendent truth at their core.

The separate Self truly melts away and collapses into unity. The Freemason now understands the symbolism of the fellowship enjoyed by the Masonic Order, as a representation that all the world's people are one, regardless of any differences which might meet the eye and mind. Therefore, as one would look after their own Self, the enlightened Freemason understands that they have a responsibility to maintain the health of one humanity.

The reason for the focus of charity, in all its forms, is understood as yet another way of facilitating this. Freemasonry looks out to the world by offering direct help, and by assisting those who wish to take the path of initiation to find the secrets of themselves in order that they might open their hearts and minds to the rest of mankind and be the best use they can be throughout their lives.

It can be seen, then, that the Royal Arch transforms the views of the Freemason by revealing the true aims of the whole system, which in turn transforms the whole of the Freemason. After much time using the tools of their own faculties to carve away the fragments of the psyche that have previously obscured it from view, a shining jewel is uncovered from within, its radiance benefiting the whole of the organism and beyond. This hidden treasure that awaits us, encased deep within ourselves, is the true reward that lies at the end of the journey in stone.

NEW BOOK *from* Lewis Masonic

THE WINDING STAIRCASE
A VISUAL JOURNEY THROUGH THE HISTORY AND SYMBOLISM OF THE CRAFT AND ROYAL ARCH DEGREES
HUW PRITCHARD

The Winding Staircase looks at some of the images and objects used in Masonic ritual to illuminate the Freemason's journey of self-discovery. It examines how Freemasonry's use of symbolism and allegory can provide the Freemason with tools to assist him in both facing the challenges of his everyday life and in exploring his spirituality. By looking at the development of these symbols and ritual objects and by the examination of contemporary images it also sheds light on the evolution of English Freemasonry itself.

The richly illustrated chapters demonstrate the evolution of Masonic ritual from an initial two-degree system to the Three Craft Degrees and Royal Arch Masonry known to us today.

Paperback • 96pp • illustrated • ISBN 9780853184959 • £12.99

ABOUT THE AUTHOR

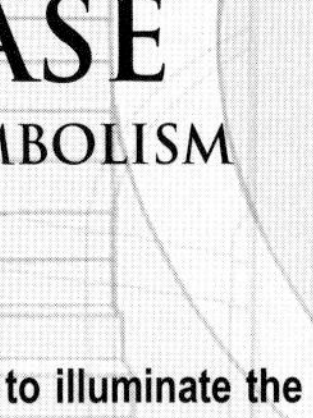

Huw Pritchard was born in 1960 and studied French and Italian at University before qualifying as a Chartered Accountant in 1986. After 25 years working for the Edmond de Rothschild Group, latterly as Chief Financial Officer of the London group, he left to study for a Master's degree in Art History and Art World Practice at Christie's Education in London. His Masters thesis examining Masonic symbolism from an art historical perspective formed the basis of this first book. He is a Fellow of the Royal Society of Arts and is a fourth generation Freemason, having been initiated by his father in 1982.

Available now from:
Lewis Masonic • Riverdene Business Park • Molesey Road
Hersham • Surrey KT12 4RG
Tel: 01932 266635 • Fax: 01932 266636
Visit us online at: www.lewismasonic.com

Lewis Masonic

NEW BOOK *from* Lewis Masonic

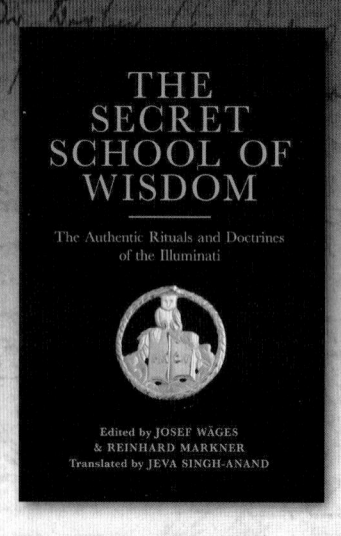

THE SECRET SCHOOL OF WISDOM

THE AUTHENTIC RITUALS AND DOCTRINES OF THE ILLUMINATI

EDITED BY JOSEF WAGES & REINHARD MARKNER

TRANSLATED BY JEVA SINGH-ANAND

The Secret School of Wisdom - The Authentic Rituals and Doctrines of the Illuminati is a pioneering text, a full working manual of the Order, and an astounding insight into the world's most intriguing secret society.

For more than two hundred years, the world has held a prejudiced view of the Illuminati. Much has been claimed for and against the Order - its name synonymous with secrecy, intrigue, and mystery in the modern context, despite a poverty of concrete evidence in the English language. Little has been said about the factual structure and development through its life cycle. This new book is a ground-breaking text. It marks the first time that a comprehensive ritual book for the society has been re-assembled. Every degree, its instruction and associated texts, has been included and assembled in chronological order of progression. The reader is guided along the same path as many of Germany's most enlightened men, as they were in the years immediately prior to the French Revolution.

Much of this material has never been published - let alone translated into English. Supplemental texts are included to gain further historical insight into the Order and all documents have been checked for accuracy with the original archival texts.

Hardback • 478pp • illustrated • ISBN 9780853184935 • £25.00

Available now from:
Lewis Masonic • Riverdene Business Park • Molesey Road
Hersham • Surrey KT12 4RG
Tel: 01932 266635 • Fax: 01932 266636
Visit us online at: www.lewismasonic.com

Lewis Masonic